PAW PRINTS
ON THE KITCHEN FLOOR

Lead Author: Kim Lengling

Book Cover Design: @Unikedesign

Publisher: Page Turner Publishing, LLC

ISBN: 979-8-9908819-2-1 (Paperback)

ISBN: 979-8-9908819-3-8 (ebook)

INTRODUCTION

We are blessed when a presence graces our homes with joy and unconditional love in the rush of everyday life and the noise of responsibilities. It is the presence of our furry friends, whose paw prints mark our kitchens' floors and leave imprints upon our souls.

Welcome to Paw Prints on the Kitchen Floor, a unique and heartfelt journey that delves into the extraordinary bond between humans and their pets. Each story in this book is shared by a pet parent and told in their own words, creating a diverse and unique collection of furry tales that represent a wide range of pet experiences.

The stories will share funny anecdotes and tender moments shared between pets and their pet parents, discovering the remarkable ability of animals to uplift our spirits, heal our wounds, and ignite hope within our hearts.

From mischievous kittens to the devotion of aging dogs, each story is a powerful testament to the transformative power of love in its purest, most unconditional form.

But "Paw Prints on the Kitchen Floor" is more than just a collection of heartwarming tales; it celebrates the lessons our furry companions teach us.

They teach us to embrace the world's wonders with open hearts, eyes, and open minds.

Their ability to live in the present moment inspires us to cherish life's simple pleasures and find beauty in everyday life.

Prepare to embark on an emotional journey filled with laughter, tears, and moments of profound insight. These stories will bring joy and laughter to your heart, leaving you uplifted and entertained.

Whether you are a seasoned pet parent, a devoted animal lover, or simply someone who delights in the magic of our furry friends, 'Paw Prints on the Kitchen Floor' promises to touch your heart, uplift your spirits, and reaffirm your belief in the transformative power of love.

FOREWORD

 Hey there! I'm Dexter, and yep! I'm a dog. A seven-year-old Belgian Malinois/Mastiff Mix, to be exact.

I know what you're thinking. How can a dog write a foreword? I'm not even sure what that word means, but my Lady Mum says I'm really smart, and she knows how to type. So here we are, doing this Foreword thing.

I'm sposed to tell ya a little about me. So here we go.

I've been living with my Lady Mum for a while now, and I know I changed her life in a good way. Do you want to know how I know? Because she told me so. She says she is blessed because I make her laugh and give good snuggles. I also like taking her on lots of walks cuz exercise is good for humans. But I like walks too cuz I get to sniff everything!

So what is this book is about? Well, it's about humans, that's you, reading this book, sharing how their pets, whether dogs like me, cats who think they rule their homes, or even super smart, caring horses, have brought love and goodness into their human's life.

We all have jobs to do for our humans—well, we have lots of jobs to do—and the stories in this book will show you how important our jobs are for our humans.

Take Asti the cat. She's in this book. She was the perfect Party Host!

Then there's Thunder, the horse who taught her girl-human about trust and patience.

There are plenty of dog stories in this book, too—dogs like me who were sick and scared when I was rescued from the animal shelter, dogs that wag their tails with excitement to see their humans walk through the door and dogs that can help a broken heart. You get the idea.

Part of our job is to remind you humans to live in the moment. Look at and appreciate the little things, like a good belly rub, a long walk, or a snuggle on the couch.

It doesn't matter if you have a dog, cat, horse, or any other furry or feathered friend; the point of each story is the same: we, as your pets, do our best to love you with all our heart for our entire life.

We try to teach you about unconditional love, how to laugh at the silliness that can happen in a day, and, at times, how to give you the companionship that no one else can.

We're only around for a short time, so we do our best to give you all the love we can. You know we are more than just animals, right? We're your family!

Furry hugs to ya,

Dexter

p.s. My Lady Mum helped me with some of the bigger words.

"Rescued is my favorite breed." - Anonymous

Alice

ALICE

By Angela Eller

It was the fall of 2016, and my husband and I had just celebrated our first wedding anniversary over the summer. The transition into autumn has always been a favorite of mine, and I remember September being particularly beautiful that year, with sunny days and crisp temperatures.

One Sunday, I celebrated at a friend's bridal shower with an outdoor tea party. I recall my friends in attendance inquiring when my husband and I would add a new addition to our family. At the time, they weren't implying a pregnancy; everyone wondered when we would get our first dog together.

I quickly dismissed these insinuations and told everyone that I did not feel quite ready yet, that we had many upcoming travel plans, that I was working long and sporadic shifts at my job, and that we were enjoying our easy and carefree newly married life. When the time was right, we would adopt. Little did I know that the very next day, my heart and our lives would be forever changed.

My husband came across an online post from The ANNA Shelter featuring three small dogs that had recently been rescued and were looking for new homes. We had gone to the shelter a few times before to meet the featured dogs, but by the time we got there, the dogs were already adopted and into their fur-ever homes, so we took those instances as signs that it was not our time yet.

I assumed this day would be no different. I figured these dogs would also be adopted by the time we got out of work and could make it to the shelter, but I agreed to go along anyway.

We walked into the shelter, and much to our surprise, the dogs were still there. A staff member quickly escorted us to a visitation room. They brought the dogs to meet us, and all it took was a moment's look, and my husband immediately fell in love with one of the little girls.

She was so small and thin, her fur blemished and shaved down from allergies, fleas, and urine burns. Her giant brown eyes seemed to pop out of her little head when she looked up at us.

We didn't know much about her; the shelter knew very little about her history, her previous living situation, her age, or even what breed she might be, but we knew she was ours. And so, we signed papers, donated to the shelter, and headed out with our new dog-ter.

We worried that separating one from the pack may not be in her best interest, but the shelter staff assured us that our little dog was the pack's alpha and would be fine independently, soaking up all the attention.

We were happy to oblige, and fortunately, another woman had come in behind us to adopt the other two remaining dogs from the rescue. We exchanged contact information to keep in touch and reunite the dogs in the future.

We headed to the pet store first to get everything she would need for her new life with us: kibble, food and water bowls, a leash and collar, a few toys, and a soft bed (which ultimately became decorative; at night, she sleeps next to my head in bed).

And then, we headed home on our new adventure. We settled on the name Alice, as I have always loved the story of Alice in Wonderland, and the name seemed to suit our own Alice's curious little personality.

She took no time at all to acclimate to her new surroundings, running straight into the house and jumping onto the couch to settle in and nap. She was at peace, she knew she was home, and I knew she had our hearts.

With proper diet, grooming, love, and care, Alice resembled her namesake, pretty and dainty. Her fur grew soft and white, her giant expressive eyes were one of her best features, and her darling wiggly waterspout tail emulated joy. She is beautiful, inside and out.

One year after her adoption, we threw a "Gotcha Day" party at our home with family, friends, and fur friends, and, of course, invited the other two dogs from the rescue to celebrate. We could tell the dogs recognized one another still. They all looked happy and healthy and greeted each other with wiggly tails.

It is often said that you don't rescue a dog; a dog rescues you, which couldn't be more accurate for Alice. She has taught us lessons in love, patience, and living each day with a happy and grateful heart.

Eight years later, we are still enjoying adventures together with Alice. Since we brought her home, she has had many adventures with us, including vacationing in the Outer Banks, spending days on Presque Isle, and moving into our forever dream home.

In the fall of 2020, she became a "big" sister to her human brother, Charlie, who weighed more than she did when he was a few months old. And yet she has been gentle and patient with him as he's grown from an unaware infant into a mischievous toddler and now a rambunctious little boy. They are becoming the best of friends and have developed common interests like walks outside, rides in the red wagon, and goldfish crackers.

I've always appreciated Alice's innate sense of those around her. She has comforted people in many circumstances and helped heal the hearts of other family members who have had to say goodbye to their dogs.

I know that Alice was the first to know of my pregnancy. She never left my side when I was not feeling well. I was also diagnosed with breast cancer in 2023 at the age of 32, and as difficult as that was for our entire family to face, Alice was steadfast and solid in her unconditional love for us all, and she made many days better and brighter with her presence.

Coming home from long doctor appointments to her happy wagging tail and kisses, anxiously awaiting results with her on my lap to calm my nerves, recovering from the surgeries, and always having her curled up next to me, she was my constant. I will forever be grateful for her presence. I will continue to try to repay her for all she has done for me, including but not limited to now cooking her homemade meals and treats to improve her kidney health, giving her lots of pets and snuggles, occasionally spoiling her with ice cream, and taking her along on her favorite adventures.

Looking back, the day before I met Alice, I was unprepared for how much would change and whether my heart would be ready for her. But now I realize I am blessed that she came into my life, stole my heart, and changed everything.

So much has happened over time, and though it is good to look back to see how far we have come, I am even more eager to look ahead to the future.

Another Alice once said, "It's no use going back to yesterday because I was a different person then." (Lewis Carroll, 1865)

"As anyone who has ever been around a cat for any length of time well knows. Cats have enormous patience with the limitations of the human kind."

Cleveland Amory

Asti

ENTERTAINING WITH ASTI

By Carrie Carter

"Welcome!"

Asti may not have spoken English, but everyone understood what her meow meant.

She stood inside the living room at the front door, greeting the guests as they arrived at the party. Her short midnight black tail shot up in the air. Everyone paused to stroke her uber-soft fur and say hello. They admired her rounded face and petite body—all 6 pounds of it.

Asti was a special cat.

I know; I can hear your eyes rolling as you read that. Every owner thinks their cat is special, and this is true because every cat IS special.

But Asti was exceptional. Yes, she was more special than the rest. I'm not simply saying that because of how we met the first time. I stepped outside my house, late for work on a sticky early June morning. General malaise and irritation clung to my skin. I did not want to go to work.

Suddenly, a kitten bounded onto my porch. The tiny fuzzball crawled up my leg, onto my shoulder, and fell asleep.

Worries about work dissolved immediately, and my heart swelled by the cuteness of it all. I knew right then that Asti was an exceptional feline.

No, that's not what made her extraordinary. Any cat can steal your heart upon meeting.

I'm also not saying she's the best because her favorite evening activity was to play chase.

I chased her around the rooms until she hid behind the curtains, her tail swishing outside the confines of the fabric. She chirped from behind the panels, not quite understanding the *hide* part of hide and seek.

"Where's Asti?" I mused.

At the sound of my voice, she'd come bounding out. The roles flipped, and now I was the one being chased. We'd continue until one or both of us grew tired. Finally, we would settle on the sofa for a cuddle. Her petite head rubbed against my face, getting tiny black cat hairs up my nose as her purrs filled every inch of the room.

That's not what makes her the number one kitty. Any cat can frolic with their human friend or snuggle on the couch.

Nor was it her loud vocal sounds and her keen hearing that ranked her above other cats.

Her ears would twitch as my car approached the house, about four blocks away. At the sound, the meows began, long, loud, and incessant. By the time I pulled into the driveway, her tiny kitty vocal cords would be tired, and her voice would be hoarse. Without fail, she would greet me at the door.

No, Asti was an exception because she embraced the role of the perfect party host.

I'm certain when I wasn't around, she turned on the TV to observe Martha Stewart on her talk show. Asti took notes and memorized advice about how to greet guests, what food to serve, and when to cut someone off from alcohol. She vowed to be the best cat host ever.

You see, Asti loved parties, be they shindigs, soirees, galas, or just a casual get-together.

She enjoyed being around people. Whether they had been long, fast friends or just met that afternoon, it didn't matter.

Two annual parties appeared on my calendar, one to dye Easter eggs and one to carve Halloween pumpkins. Gazing at the moon, sniffing the humidity levels in the air, and eyeing the sudden high quantity of wine bottles and bags of potato chips entering the house, she knew party time was approaching.

While the cast of characters changed with each gathering, and sometimes the address was different, they all went down in a similar fashion.

Before each party, the house must be cleaned and prepped, and it must have a faint smell of lemons or maybe lavender blowing in a spring breeze. While Asti may not have used her paws to wipe down countertops or wash and dry the dishes, she gathered any

20

random, loose socks and buried them in the cat box. She swatted at the mini-blind slats to remove any dust that might have collected; of course, the amount of dust never failed to impress.

Once the additional chairs were out for the guests, she inspected them, lying on each one to make sure the people would find them comfortable. She rearranged items on the table until they were more aesthetically pleasing. She had a sharp eye, knowing which item needed to be removed and pushed onto the floor. A flower might be yanked out of the vase onto the floor, and the arrangement went from passable to a masterpiece.

Her whiskers curved forward in anticipation of the people gathering in the house, offering scratches under the chin and bites of party food snuck to her when I wasn't watching.

Before the event started, while I sat on the porch drinking lemonade and waiting for the first guests, she galloped to anyone walking on the sidewalk. She meowed, inviting them to the party, but having not been around her and unaware of what she said, they merely smiled.

"It's almost time, Asti. Let's go in," I called out to her.

She raced through the front door and jumped on the kidney-shaped coffee table to take a quick nap before the festivities. All the preparation had worn her out.

A knock on the door snapped her out of sleep. Her ears twitched, and she lifted her head—another knock. Trotting to the door, she stood there, annoyed I hadn't already opened it to let people in.

Time to festivate!

As each person arrived, she said hello, playing the part of the perfect hostess. She led them to the dining room table, where they could choose their beverage. Another person arrived and sent her scurrying back to the front door.

Once people had their drinks, they moved to the porch or the living room. Here, the genuine fun began. Asti tested every lap, making sure she warmed the legs before moving to the next person. No one could ignore her.

As for friends who had cat allergies, they weren't invited. Such an unfortunate result, but what are you going to do?

Asti moved about the room, person to person. She never left anyone out; she didn't want to hurt anyone's feelings. When she reached the last person, she would start again.

The people would coo at her and take photos. They marveled at her good looks and outgoing personality.

Asti was the cat version of Martha Stewart if you took away the cooking, craft-making, gardening, and going to prison.

When the wine in the glass got dangerously low, she would sniff the rim, look at me, and demand that I pour more inky liquid into it. She would have done it herself if she had opposable thumbs and the strength to lift a wine bottle.

As we both got older, the number of parties dwindled. My friends came over less frequently as their jobs became more demanding; some had kids, and everyone got lazy.

Eventually, the parties stopped altogether.

Asti lived a long, fruitful 18-year-old life before passing. The memories of egg-dying get-togethers and pumpkin-carving gatherings flashed through my mind. Asti commanded the room at these parties. I recall them with a sense of wistfulness and wish for one more party with Asti as the host.

"Dogs have a way of finding the people who need them and filling an emptiness we didn't ever know we had."

Thom Jones

Brodie

BRODIE: THE OLD SOUL

By Maureen Scanlon

I think it's amazing how animals pick us! No, really, I've seen it time and again; they end up with the people they come to save with unconditional love.

My furry baby, Brodie, an Australian Shepherd, started as a "trial" for my daughter, Jordania, and her boyfriend at the time. See, she got Brodie before leaving for college, and they were going to "share" custody while she was away at college.

Lucky for me (and honestly, for her, too), she decided to break up with him right after he dropped her off. And so, Brodie, an 8-week-old little floofy boy, became mine permanently.

I always felt like Brodie knew me. It was as if he could read my mind and heart. I was myself, getting out of yet another toxic relationship with a narcissist.

I would sit at night crying, wondering what was wrong with me and why I was so unlovable. Brodie and his chunky 15-pound chihuahua sister, Jade, would sit with me and lick my tears and reassure me that I was, in fact, very lovable in their eyes!

It started my epiphany to recognize that dogs are teachers, social workers, angels, and unconditionally loving souls. I found my love for myself through their eyes!

My journey and life took a new trajectory of helping others "become their own best friend." I wrote books for the first time without knowing I could, and I started a life coaching business to help others find their worth and confidence.

26

Brodie was like an old soul, a calm grandpa energy but with an occasional howl in the backyard. Perhaps he had some of his wolf ancestry that needed to appear now and then.

He was so patient with our other dog, Jade. She was certainly annoying at times and would flip over between his paws as he was lying down and nibble on his cheek. He'd let it happen for a few minutes and then put his big paw on her head to say, "Ok, that's enough for today, little sis."

Brodie and Jade loved their walks together. He insisted on being in the front to lead both Jade and me. I still think it was his nature always to protect his family. He'd even lay between me and the bedroom door or on the landing outside my room to keep an eye on the front door.

Brodie started limping regularly and was diagnosed with Hip Dysplasia, which is common in shepherd breeds. I bought assist harnesses, braces, CBD, Joint Chews, and even a massager for nightly massages. I wanted to do anything I could to relieve his pain.

He tried so hard to be sure to go outside to the bathroom and NEVER had an accident up to the day he passed. I even tried a wheelchair for his back legs, but he did not want anything to do with that. He had a lot of pride and never wanted me to see him as unable to protect me. He wanted to be there for me no matter what it took or how much pain he was in.

I remember Mother's Day, the last year of his life. He hadn't been out for a walk for some time, and I didn't want to aggravate his hip pain. I was going to take Jade out for a walk, and he went to the door and squeezed out. Even though he couldn't walk 20 steps, he still wanted to be out there with us; it's just who he was.

On December 15, 2022, I noticed his front shoulder looked swollen. Then he started limping on his front left leg. My first thought was, "Oh no, Dysplasia in his shoulder now?" I immediately took him to our veterinarian, fully expecting my predicted diagnosis to be correct. They carried him from the car on a cart and took him straight back for an X-ray.

I'll never forget when the doctor looked at me and said, "I'm so sorry; he has cancer." My mind immediately froze and couldn't or wouldn't accept the words. No, I thought, it's just arthritis; he's only 11 1/2 years old.

It is Osteosarcoma, a cancer that starts in the bone and grows until it shatters the bone.

No, no, no, please don't let this be true. Not my boy, not my protector, sweet, loving, funny, sibling-loving boy! And NOT THIS WAY!

And then, the life-shattering question we must ask is, "How long does he have?"

"Maybe a month to six weeks max," she said. I'll be honest: I hated her at that moment. It was completely unfounded, but I did. She was telling me the heart-piercing, soul-crushing words that would devastate me.

We leave with the standard prescription for Gabapentin and hope she's wrong. My denying mind said my boy would be a miracle, and we'd get ten more years. It's funny how the mind works because I'd look so hard every day after that visit for signs he was improving. I'd tell my husband, "Look, he got up easier than usual," or "I think he jogged a little bit today." That's the denial and negotiation part of grief.

In my backyard, I had two little vegetable garden beds. I called them my Jack and Jill gardens. Brodie never went into my gardens. He was so considerate; he would walk around them, and he wasn't a digger either.

A couple of days after the bad news, I went outside and saw him lying smack in the middle of my garden. He looked so happy. He was enjoying the cool soil and smiling. He was always a serious boy, and to see this joy on his face melted my heart.

Six days later, I was going to give him a bath in the shower; as I was walking him over to the bathroom, he let out a horrible scream of pain.

I had been given a dog bed that he loved and always slept on in the living room, and I took him over to it to lie down. His whimpering and obvious pain were tearing me apart. It was the moment that the bone shattered, and he wouldn't get any relief. It was December 21st, just four days before Christmas.

Everyone was visiting for the holidays. My son and daughter-in-law came straight from work. I was determined to give him the most loving sendoff I could. It would never measure up to the 11 ½ years of joy and love he gave us, but I would not let him leave in a cold Veterinarian's room.

I called around to see if someone could come to the house to help us say goodbye in his home with his people. I found the most compassionate, mobile veterinarian who was patient and understanding of what our family was experiencing. She was able to come to our home and walk through Brodie's final moments with us.

Every family member was there, and everyone got to sit with him and tell him thank you and how much they loved him. It was the most beautiful thing.

What was most heartbreaking was watching Jade's behavior. She lay next to him, wouldn't leave his side, and would lick his face. It was her way of saying she loved him and to say goodbye to her big brother.

As he fell asleep peacefully with his people around him, I know he did this his way. He chose the moment everyone would be together because that's who Brodie was; the old soul who brought everyone together with his kind eyes, bushy tail, and unconditional, protective love.

We moved from Arizona to Texas three months later.

As I was sitting in my new home, I saw him out of the corner of my eye. We've since adopted my grandson's dog, Callie, an Aussie/Border mix, and I thought it was her walking by. As I went to look for her, I noticed she was sleeping in the front room.

I knew at that moment Brodie was showing me he was still with me. It wasn't easy selling our old house because of the memories of him. As usual, he found a way to soothe and make me feel loved. His ashes and paw print are in my new office, and I often think of him. When I do, I'll see something of his, like a toy or a picture of him.

The best part is seeing characteristics in Callie similar to Brodie's when caring for Jade. It's as if Brodie passed the torch, and Callie gladly said, "I accept the mission."

Dogs are such caretakers and loving beings; I feel we aren't always worthy of them but thank goodness they believe we are!

"The greatness of a nation and its moral progress can be judged by the way its animals are treated."

Gandhi

Buddy

WHO RESCUED WHO?

By Jessica Corey

I have wanted a dog for as long as I can remember. Growing up, my family had several cats but never any dogs.

When I met my significant other, Brian, he was the opposite. He grew up with dogs only and never had a cat. Once our landlord approved our request to adopt a dog from a local shelter in the fall of 2020, our search for a new family member soon began!

Since I had no experience with dogs, Brian and I discussed how it might be best for us to look for a small, middle-aged dog. I searched several local shelter pages for dogs currently available for adoption but eventually looked at The ANNA Shelter in Erie, PA.

When we walked into the inside dog kennel area, they had a lot of large, high-energy, vocal dogs. One dog in a middle kennel was quiet, lying down with big, sad eyes. His name on the kennel said Hank.

Hank was a malnourished black dog with orange-brown colored eyebrows and areas on his chest and paws. The kennel said he was a one or two-year-old Rottweiler/Chow-Chow mix. His coloring was the same as that of a Rottweiler, and his fur length and purple spotted tongue were that of a Chow Chow.

I looked at Brian and said, "Awe, I saw Hank on their Facebook page a day or two ago! He is so cute. Look at those eyebrows!"

33

We asked a kind employee at the shelter if we could take Hank out of his kennel and into their outdoor yard. We learned during our visit that The ANNA Shelter rescued Hank from a kill shelter in Indiana. He was currently low energy because he had just been neutered and was heartworm positive. Luckily, the shelter's veterinarian, Dr. Lyon, was able to treat Hank for heartworm, and after being retested a few months after the treatment, he was heartworm negative.

After interacting with Hank in the yard for nearly 45 minutes, Brian and I went back and forth about whether Hank should become a new part of our family.

Hank was well-behaved, friendly, and laid back. The major issue in our decision was that Hank was larger than we anticipated our new family member to be, but the longer we spent time with him, the more we realized it did not matter how big he was. It truly felt like Hank was picking us by following us around and jumping on the bench we were sitting on to receive cuddles.

We filled out the paperwork and made it official! The drive home was especially exciting for Hank. He was smiling, his tongue hanging out, and he stuck his head out of the car window. I have always liked thinking of unique nicknames, so I knew I wanted to come up with a different name for Hank.

Whenever Brian and I would interact with Hank, we would find ourselves saying things like "Come here, buddy" or "Awe, good boy, buddy!" After many name options neither of us could mutually agree on, Brian says, "How about we just call him Buddy?"

I agreed but was disappointed that I could not think of something more unique than Buddy, which I have always considered one of the most common dog names. After some time, though, Buddy's nicknames grew by the day! One of his most popular and well-known nicknames is Buddernut Squash, but he also goes by Budders, Bodean, Barracuda, Buddy Bear, Sassy Boi, and My Sun.

When we got home for the first time with Buddy, Brian said he would go to our local pet supply store for a large dog crate, dog bed, dog food, collar, leash, pooper scooper, assorted treats, and a couple of new toys.

While Brian was gone, I took Buddy on his first walk around our big yard, and he loved it! Next, I took Buddy on a tour of his new home. When Buddy jumped on the couch for the first time, he walked right on top of my lap and sat. I was beginning to realize that Buddy would not be "just a dog" or a new family member; he would soon become my best friend.

Buddy was unlike many dogs. He did not beg for food; he begged for attention. Brian and I would be eating dinner, and Buddy did not care about the steak we were eating; he cared that he couldn't lay on the couch and cuddle with us.

We also learned that Buddy preferred not to be around any male who wasn't Brian. I don't like to think of Buddy's life when he was Hank because I don't think he was treated the best by men. Luckily, there isn't much of a reason for Buddy to encounter many males.

About a year after adopting Buddy, I started noticing that I was beginning to feel off emotionally. I was not responding as I usually would to texts or phone calls, feeling like everyone hated me and sad feelings in general. I was diagnosed with depression and anxiety.

Throughout the entire process, Buddy was my constant. He was happy to see me every day and be there to cuddle when that was all I felt I could do for the day. He always jumped on my lap when I cried and lay there because he knew I needed him. Buddy made me feel safe and comfortable when I didn't feel the least bit happy or like myself.

October 10th, 2024, will mark Buddy's 4th year as our adopted dog son. He loves walking around our big yard or the wooded park near our house. Having Buddy has given me a new appreciation for nature and the beauty of being outdoors during any season. Growing up, I was not a fan of snow, but having a dog in the winter is so much fun. Buddy loves eating snow and making dog snow angels.

My favorite part of the day is coming home from work, walking around the kitchen corner, and being greeted with a hug and kiss from Buddy. In the evenings, after dinner, we catch up on our favorite TV shows and cuddle as a family, with Buddy in the middle, of course.

I joke with friends and family that my sassy gene has passed on to Buddy. Buddy is vocal when he wants attention and will let you know if you aren't rubbing his stomach to his liking (Laugh. Out. Loud.) As a sassy individual myself, I am keen on this behavior and tend to egg it on (sorry, Brian).

They say getting a dog is a huge responsibility, and I have learned that to be true. They need food, water, and bathroom breaks. They have a need to chew bones, furniture, carpets, and so forth.

It is also a rewarding responsibility to have a dog. They show you such a genuine form of love, compassion, and trust. Buddy has become such an important and special part of our family. I am thankful each day for our decision to adopt him from The ANNA Shelter. Buddy has shown me what a true best friend looks like and that he was able to rescue me, too!

"Rescue: It's not just a verb. It's a promise."

Anonymous

Chico

UNDER A STURGEON MOON

By Anna Carranza

Twelve years ago, on a sweltering and humid August morning, a little shooting star changed my life forever. This tiny, mighty golden fireball was quite extraordinary. His name was Chico, and this is his story.

"How do you expect today to go?" My husband smiled before taking a long sip of coffee from his portable mug as he stood by the front door waiting for me.

I had been pacing around the kitchen, ensuring everything was ready for the big day. I hadn't slept all night thinking about this moment. There was something magical in the air. I had butterflies in my stomach.

"I think it will be very special," I responded.

He nodded. We seemed calm.

The care package was filled with pet toys and other essentials. As we left, I looked back at our little apartment and took a deep breath. This is it.

Months prior, my husband and I had decided to get a puppy, our first pet. We settled on a Yorkie since we lived in a Pasadena apartment and believed this breed would best fit our lifestyle.

I began the search with joy. I read everything I could get my hands on, explored online resources, looked at adorable pictures, researched breeds, spoke to friends and family, and prepared for the special homecoming. We eventually found a Palmdale breeder with good references.

We made a pact to play it cool, watch closely, and not make any hasty decisions. We would observe how the puppies moved and played together, look at their appearance and personality, and, most importantly, remember that one puppy would choose us. The rest would be left to faith.

The Palmdale ranch was brutally hot as we knocked on the door, wondering what would be on the other side. A lovely Filipino woman answered and welcomed us in. She had mother vibes. Destiny. A feeling of comfort and trust embraced us as we stepped into her air-conditioned home. Delicious, savory cooking smells drifted in from the kitchen.

The breeder had her daughters show us the litter in a little pen in the middle of the living room. And there they were! All these tiny little darlings. All but one had the characteristic coat of steel blue. Chico, a gorgeous silky rich golden tan color, was in the middle, looking glorious.

"He's the runt of the litter." The breeder smiled. Chico moved toward us with presence and confidence.

As he nuzzled up to me, he announced himself. *Well, hello, family. I have been waiting for you.* With his puppy breath. Unforgettable. Like baby's breath.

I mentioned it to the breeder.

"It's a bonding thing," she responded. "It's associated with pheromones and natural oils which elicit positive emotions of comfort and happiness."

His grand entrance was surreal. I never imagined anything quite so adorable. From that moment on, my heart was his. Game over.

When we left, things felt like a blur, like the euphoric feeling of falling in love. Washed with sunlight, we spoke a new language, songs came, and conversation grew more nuanced. "Thank you for choosing me," I whispered to Chico.

In the following year, Chico adjusted to his new home naturally. On his river leisure, butterflies danced around him. Pretty things consumed him. He saw beyond little nuisances, like flies and mosquitoes, saving his energy for the big dogs around our neighborhood. He felt sure he could take them on.

I kept an eye on him, worried he would get hurt because of his tiny stature. Little did I know how tough he was. I would scoop him up during our walks as he barked furiously at his much larger rivals. Luckily, there were no incidents.

Our older cat made it his priority to be Chico's protective big brother. An alliance was formed. Partners in crime. They both slept on our bed. Their sweet little snores rose and fell in sync with our shared dreams.

Chico was complex. Take our Chloe bag games, for example. I had this oversized tan Chloe bag I used as his carrier. He would snuggle deep inside and instantly go still.

We could go anywhere, anytime, and he would not be detected. It became more than a game—our pact. I took him to movie theaters, supermarkets, and events. When he came out of the Chloe bag, he was a showstopper.

His favorite activity was riding in the basket of my bicycle down the strand in Hermosa Beach, with his large ears flying in the breeze and his signature long tongue hanging out. He liked all worlds; if you listened to him, he would tell you great things.

For our family, he was an avid guard dog with might and courage, a lover, a clown, and my best little buddy.

The years pass far too quickly. I regret that I thought he would always be here. I took our time for granted.

We went for our nightly walk together the week of the Sturgeon Moon. I didn't know that it would be our last. We found a little bench to get a clear view, and he sat with me. He looked at me with the light of the moon illuminating him. I wondered why he had such deep thoughts.

My work schedule changed unexpectedly the next day when a meeting was canceled. I came home in the afternoon, unusually tired. I went to the bedroom to take a quick nap. I saw Chico on my bed. He didn't seem that different. When I awoke, I spoke to him. He looked at me with his enormous eyes and his long tongue, which, for the first time, was dark. I knew this was not good. I picked him up and carried him to the living room.

Concerned, I called my husband and told him to come home immediately.

In the next few minutes, I had a vivid out-of-body experience. It was just me and Chico. I wrapped him in a comfortable blanket, and he looked at me without fear or discomfort. I swear he looked so peaceful and just wanted me to be okay. He wanted me to be with him that day. He'd waited for me.

I love you.

Suddenly, an enormous energy surge took place, and I wrapped his body and felt his neck fall back. I fell on the couch sobbing harder than I had ever done before. The door flew open, and my husband came in. He grabbed Chico in the blanket and ran out to the vet. I heard my heart break. Everything went black.

Heavy rain poured for the next few days. I was in deep mourning and overwhelmed with emotions. We buried Chico at a pet cemetery in Calabasas under a beautiful oak tree. There is an incredible sense of peace and vibrancy there. He is surrounded by beloved cats, dogs, and even a few prize-winning horses.

I visit him often with fresh flowers and tell him about all the little ways he has inspired me. I can feel him. He has finally accepted that big dogs are his buddies and not a threat.

The last moments with Chico were a gift. I don't feel he is gone. Our bond is as strong as ever, and he is always by me—my guide, my little golden star.

"You can't change a dog's past, but you can rewrite the future." - Agnes Carass

Cooper

IN COOPER'S EYES

By Lisa Lichota

The text message said, "Buy puppy chow." We didn't have a puppy. We had a beautiful adult black lab named Molly May, and though she would most likely eat anything, I knew this wasn't for her. Then, the photo came: my hubby holding a little fawn and white colored puppy. My heart exploded. Who was this little creature, and was he really ours? The workday could not end quickly enough. I needed to meet him.

I bought puppy chow and drove home to meet our Cooper - as the years passed, sometimes known as Coopie, Coopie Doopie Doo, and maybe even Turkey Bird. He was amazing. He had been rescued by a friend who contacted my husband and said, "I have someone you need to meet." It was love at first sight. That's how he came to be our bestest boy.

Our Lab, Molly, tolerated him, then welcomed him, and, with time, loved him unconditionally. We have always been the proud parents of Labrador Retrievers, and always females.

Coop was not a lab; we didn't know what he was, and we didn't care. At his first vet appointment, we labeled him a boxer mix because they needed to fill the box for "breed."

I felt a unique and almost familiar bond when I first met, held, and kissed him. Looking into his eyes, I saw something I had only seen once before. He looked at me like Lacy, my first-ever dog, had looked at me. We imprinted. I was his person. He was my dog. He was a mommy's boy.

As the first couple of months passed, I started to look online for pictures of dogs that resembled Cooper, and it didn't take long to

47

discover that we had ourselves a little Pit Bull, which is a label given to several breeds or mixes of those breeds.

This came before the current wave of Pit Bull adoration and popularity. I did a good deal of reading and realized we were in for a treat because pit bulls are a wonderful non-breed that brings more love and joy than anyone could ever imagine.

He was a true love bug. For the first year, he chose to sleep lengthwise on top of one of us. He had to be touching or snuggling us. As he grew and filled out, he began to look more like his ancestry. He was terribly handsome, and he knew it.

Cooper fit perfectly into our little world. We live next door to my in-laws, so he always had four adoring servants who would spoil him beyond measure. He would go to work next door with his grandpa and help keep an eye on the shop. This would entail shredding every piece of cardboard into tiny pieces. This brought him great joy, and it's how he earned his paycheck (and kept Grandpa busy).

He also kept a close eye on the yard. He especially loved to help with yard work on the property, and Grandpa would spoil him with tractor rides. Most days, he had the arduous task of assisting Grandma with the security of the property. This would mean a long, watchful walk around the entire property. He had to keep everyone safe and keep Grandma in shape. Another essential duty was to monitor Sparkie, the shop cat. He affectionately handled this matter.

At night, he would curl up on our bed and sleep the deep, peaceful sleep of a dog who enjoyed his life and loved his people. Pits are much more cold-blooded than Labs, so when he would burrow his body head-first under the covers, I would giggle and make him pop his nose out for air. In his mind, he could never be too warm or too close to his mommy. I lived for it!

Cooper didn't know he was a dog. He didn't lie on the floor; he lounged on a chair, the couch, or our bed. He didn't enjoy being at floor level, which was obvious at times when he would climb onto a dining room chair after dinner to be eye-level with us, never begging for food or sniffing around, just sitting with his people, loving us with his eyes.

Occasionally, I would have my gal pals over for a girls' night. He loved girls' night with his whole Pittie heart. The girls would spoil him and give him so many pets. He would slyly work his way around the table, getting all the attention, but would inevitably find a way to climb up on a chair and join us at eye level.

For no apparent reason, I deemed it scarf night one special evening, and each friend arrived wearing a scarf. By 10 pm, Cooper was in a chair at the table with his cute little head wrapped in a red scarf. He was in his glory. He welcomed photos of his big night, and his eyes showed sheer contentment.

During Cooper's lifetime, I had a few different surgeries. Cooper would be my watchful nurse, compassionate companion, and the best medicine each time. After I had foot surgery, he lounged at the bottom of the couch next to the bandaged body part, staring into my eyes and healing me with love. He stayed near in case I needed him.

Being dutiful and loyal were characteristics he took seriously. The next major surgery was due to a fall in my kitchen, a fall in which I tripped over Cooper and damaged my shoulder. He didn't exactly comprehend that I was all torn up because he had chosen an unlikely napping spot, and his mommy was clumsy and always moved about the kitchen too fast.

However, after the surgery, he took care of me like a semi-guilty party should. Even then, I reminded him of what a good boy he was, easily forgetting what had happened to land me in this mess in the first place. In Cooper's eyes, I could see empathy and concern. That's all that mattered.

Although he was a big (medium-sized), bad (sweet) Pit Bull, Coopie had some fears. He did not like loud noises. He did not like most strange men. He sometimes even had issues with the outdoors. He liked to be outside, but only in optimal weather. Even a slight breeze could sometimes make him squint his brown eyes and tremble a bit.

He also acted as if raindrops were acid falling from the sky. He hated even the gentlest rain. Unlike our former water-loving Labs, we were learning that Pitties frequently detested water on their bodies.

No, thank you, Mother Nature. When we would be outside under these despicable conditions, I would say, "Coopie-doobie-doo, everything is fine. You're a big, brave boy." He would prove me wrong. He would scurry to the door to be taken inside, retreating to his custom-made kennel in our living room, referred to as Coopie's Condo. We spoiled him, and in return, he loved us. What an amazing arrangement.

One of Cooper's and my favorite activities was sitting on the deck on beautiful spring, summer, and fall days. He enjoyed this, but unlike any other dog I have known, he enjoyed it backward. Backward? Yes. I would sit on the bottom step of the deck looking over the property and sky, and my beloved Cooper would sit down on the sidewalk, facing me, nose-to-nose, and stare into my eyes.

The whole world was right there: grass, trees, clouds, bugs, birds, butterflies, and maybe even a distant groundhog, but none of that mattered to him. I mattered to him more than anything on earth. In Cooper's eyes, I was his world. Nothing has ever made me feel this way. The love in Cooper's eyes will forever remain one of my greatest blessings.

When I lost my sweet boy one month before the pandemic shutdown, I lost the love of my life. But my life was enhanced by all our days together, and I will be forever grateful for that. When I hopefully one day arrive in heaven, I can't wait to look into Cooper's eyes and say, "There's my bestest boy!"

"A dog doesn't care if you're rich or poor.

smart or dumb.

Give him your heart and he'll give you his."

Milo Gathema

Dexter

THE CASE OF THE MISSING CIABATTA ROLLS

By Kim Lengling

It was one of those days. I was running late for work and hurriedly said goodbye to Dexter, my newly adopted and anxious dog.

I had planned a three-day weekend when I adopted and brought Dexter home. I did my best to make him feel comfortable and safe, but he still showed signs of anxiety when I would do a practice run of leaving the house.

I had to return to work, so I dog-proofed the house and kept Dexter in the kitchen for the first few days he was on his own. I am glad I did!

In the first week, I would return home from work to find the food and water bowls overturned and the water and food spread out across the kitchen floor.

One day, when I returned home and walked in the back door, I was not surprised to see the same scenario, but one thing was different.

A once full bag of Ciabatta rolls lay torn open on the floor, with one roll left. It looked as if a minor crime had occurred.

Looking for Dexter, I spot him in the corner of the dining room, head drooping in guilt and his eyes avoiding mine. It was a classic case of a bread heist gone wrong, with Dexter as the prime suspect.

I knew it was my fault for leaving food on the counter, especially with a newly adopted dog. I couldn't feel angry with him. Instead,

I picked up the bag with the remaining roll and assured Dexter he was not in trouble. At the same time, I was mentally preparing myself to have a sick dog.

Later that evening, Dexter hopped up on the couch and began digging at one of the cushions. "Dexter, No. You're going to ruin the cushion, bud." With persistence, he kept digging. Realizing something was in there, I put my hand between the cushions and, low and behold! A Ciabatta roll!

Amused, I couldn't help but laugh. "You've hidden them? Okay, it looks like I am going on a Ciabatta Roll hunt. Do you want to show me where you've hidden the rest?" I asked, half expecting a response.

Thinking a game was about to begin, Dexter jumped from the couch and looked at me with bright eyes and tail wagging, but no answer to my question was forthcoming.

With a sigh and determination, I began the hunt. Staying in the living room, I checked the recliner—another roll hidden under the seat cushion. I scour the room, my eyes catching sight of something sticking out of the dirt in one of my potted plants. You guessed it, another roll, half buried in the pot.

And yet another roll was found beneath the dog bed. That is four of the five missing Ciabatta rolls accounted for. The suspense was building as I wondered where the last one could be.

After going through the house and being unable to find the last roll, I assumed he had eaten at least one.

I kept a close eye on him throughout the evening. He seemed fine, with no signs of a tummy ache. I decided to chalk this day up as a learning experience.

As the day ended, I completed my nighttime routine and crawled into bed. Trying to get comfortable, I felt something under my pillow. There it was! The final Ciabatta roll! All five are now accounted for. I couldn't help but chuckle at the absurdity of the situation.

After a quick cleanup of crumbs, I crawled back into bed, thinking, "What is this dog going to get up to next?"

As the days passed, I was cautious not to leave food on the counter. I had learned my lesson. Or had I?

Another day and another hurried morning. Returning home from work, I found an empty bread loaf pan on the kitchen floor. Once again, Dexter is sitting in a corner of the dining room, head hanging low. I couldn't help but feel a mix of frustration and amusement at his antics.

"Dexter, what in the world! How did you reach that?"

An entire loaf of banana bread, which I had baked that morning, was missing. Shaking my head, I resigned myself to finding a mess and again began the hunt for hidden baked goods.

The search did not last long. Between the couch cushions, I found the loaf of banana bread. I was impressed—the loaf was intact, with hardly a mess to clean! Dexter's hiding skills were improving, but I couldn't help but wonder how he managed to get the loaf in the first place.

Those were the only two times Dexter snagged and buried baked goods throughout the house. I've never quite figured out why he did that on those two days, but he seems to be over it.

But a new quirk of his began to emerge. Dexter felt he needed to move the recliner, so it faced and was up against the front window. I could see how the chair's position would give him a good view of who came and went in the driveway.

Now, folks, this chair is not small or light; it is a large recliner that faces the living room, as most chairs do. But several days in a row, I returned home from work to find it turned around and facing the window that looked out onto the front yard and driveway.

Each day, with a sigh, I would turn the chair to face the living room.

But again, when I returned home from work, I saw the chair turned around and facing the window. I wondered how this dog could turn this big chair to the perfect position for viewing the coming and going of the outside world.

This game of Let's Move the Chair continued for a couple of weeks until I decided to leave the chair facing the window. Is Dexter happy not to have the chore of turning the chair each day? I think he is.

Am I happy not to have the chore of turning the chair to face the room each day? Yes, I am.

Dexter has been with me for a few years, and we've adjusted to each other and all our quirks.

On occasion, someone asks why I have a chair facing the front window instead of facing the room as a chair typically would, I say, "That's Dexter's watching chair," and leave it at that.

"As every cat owner knows.

nobody owns a cat." - Ellen Perry

Diamond

MY BEST FRIEND

By Randi Lee Bowslaugh

"Please, mom!" I beg.

"No!" Mom says.

"Please, please, please. It can be an early birthday present."

"Your birthday isn't for six more months."

"A super early present. Look at the picture, pleeeeeease."

"Fine, but it has to be a male; they are cheaper to fix."

"Thank you, thank you, thank you, thank you!" I yell as I give my mom a huge hug.

With my mom's note, I walk to school and head straight for my French teacher's classroom.

His cat had three kittens the week before, which he offered to the students. We had to get our parents' permission, bring a note, and have them available to pick up the kittens when they were old enough. He brought pictures of the kittens; they were all adorable, but one stood out to everyone. The kitten was white with the strangest black markings, which the teacher called Elmer. Everyone wanted that kitten.

I handed my note to the teacher and went to class while anxiously awaiting the final answer: if I could get one of the kittens. We had one cat at home, Tigger, who I loved dearly, but he was my mom's cat, not mine. The new kitten would be my own.

Everyone was on the edge of their seats when the teacher announced who would take the kittens home. He said since only one male was in the litter, I had to take the white and black kitten everyone wanted. I was over the moon! That was the one I wanted, but I wasn't sure because my mom had been so picky about it being a male cat.

When I finally got to bring the kitten home, I chose the name Diamond because of the facial markings. My brother teased me, saying that Diamond is not a boy cat name, but I didn't care; I knew it suited this kitten.

My mom fell in love with the little fluff ball as soon as she saw it, but then she gave me a strange look. "This isn't a male cat," she said.

"What are you talking about? My teacher said this was the only male cat." I replied.

She held the kitten and took another look. "This is definitely a female cat. I don't know what your teacher looked at when he said it was male."

"But I love her!"

"I know, that's the problem now. I guess we have a female cat." My mom sighed, snuggling Diamond closer. Even though she was annoyed that this was not a male cat, Diamond had already become part of the family. Even Tigger liked having her around.

***

I have to get out of here. I need to hide. Get upstairs, get to my room; my bed will be safe.

I crawl under my blanket, yanking it over my head, tears beginning to form when a plop at the end of the bed makes me flinch. Something was moving towards me when I heard it.

Purrrr.

Lowering the blanket, I see that Diamond has come to lie on my chest. She is always around when I need her and has a sixth sense about it.

Diamond makes herself comfortable and stares at me. To get my attention, she rubs her forehead against my chin. I smile as I begin to pet her. She loves it when I scratch behind her ear.

Eventually, the yelling in the living room quiets, but I still don't want to venture out. Luckily, I don't need to, so long as I have Diamond with me, I know I will be okay.

***

Only two months to go, and I'm big as a balloon. I waddle like a penguin, can't get up from the floor, and want this baby out of me!

Diamond is by my side, as always. No matter how big I get, she purrs and sits with me. She curls up on my belly when I lay down on my side. The baby kicks, and Diamond continues to purr. The baby pets the cat before they are even born.

I'm finally home from the hospital. I put the car seat on the ground and let Diamond sniff. She is so curious about what this new little thing is. It smells like me but isn't. Diamond boops the baby's foot with the top of her head, and the baby smiles at her.

Diamond sleeps close to the baby as she grows as if protecting her.

When the baby learns to crawl, Diamond isn't sure if she likes this. The baby will chase Diamond, but Diamond doesn't hiss; she walks slowly, just out of reach, playing with the baby and moving just enough to encourage the baby to crawl further.

She is standing on things now, her eyes glued to Diamond. Diamond stares right back. Diamond is never far from the baby.

At times, the baby reaches her arm out but can't quite reach Diamond. Diamond rubs up against my leg, trying to provoke the baby to get back down and crawl toward her. She'll then walk away as if saying, *"If you want to pet me, you need to walk to me."*

The baby pulls herself up to the chair to stand again. Diamond stops walking and sits, staring, tail swishing, waiting. One tiny hand comes off the chair; there is a little wobble before standing tall with no hands.

I sit a few steps away, petting Diamond. We are both waiting now. The baby and Diamond's eyes lock. A heartbeat later, the baby takes their first step.

I smile and continue to pet Diamond. The baby takes another step, another, and the last step before falling beside Diamond.

I tell the baby how amazing she is. Still, the only thing that matters is Diamond's praise through rubbing up against the baby and purring. The baby smiles. Diamond purrs. They are best friends, just like Diamond and me.

***

It has been 19 years, multiple moves, marriage, children, and ups and downs, and Diamond has been by my side through it all.

She turned cat haters into cat lovers and never let a dog take her space.

Now she is growing tired. She struggles to reach the litter box, so I place puppy pads around it. Sometimes, she has accidents, and I clean her up. I built her a staircase to get up into bed. She still loves to be petted and watch the birds outside.

One evening, she doesn't want to eat. My heart breaks into a thousand pieces. I opened a can of tuna, her favorite, but it did not interest her. I know this is it. I don't want it to be, but I know it is.

She walks to her new fish pillow and gets comfortable. I lay beside her, talking with her and petting her. She still softly purrs, and tears well in my eyes. She slips towards the floor, and I fix her on the pillow.

I lay on the floor beside her all night, eventually falling asleep. When I wake in the morning, she is gone. My husband has moved her and placed her in a carrier to prepare for the drive to the Humane Society.

I can't believe she is gone. I know she had a good, long life. She made my life better, and I miss her every day. I tell my grandson stories about her and keep her alive in my home as she is always alive in my heart.

Because a Diamond is a girl's best friend.

"It's rewarding beyond words to rescue a dog from the shelter and have that dog become part of your family." - Jenna Morasca

Freddy

FREDDY'S DAY

By Randi Lee Bowslaugh

I breathe on Mom's face, waiting for her to open her eyes. She pushes me away and rolls over. I jump off the bed, look at the closed door, stomp my foot, and look back at her. She's trying to ignore me. I stomp both my front feet, and she finally rolls over.

"Fine!" she grumbles and gets out of bed.

She opens the door, and I saunter out and crawl onto the crouch.

"Seriously, Fred? You acted like you needed to go pee." Mom lets my brother and sister outside. "Come on, Freddy. Go outside and go pee." She stares at me, trying to coax me into the backyard. I don't want to go into the backyard; I will wait for my walk. "Fine, then you can just wait, silly boy."

Mom finally finishes her breakfast and is dressed. I dance around to get her attention. It is my favorite time of day, walk time. Mom puts on our leashes and takes us for a walk. I miss it when it was just my walk, but I am still the leader.

We go around, and I sniff the grass, trees, flowers, and all the random things on the ground. Mom stops me from eating the bread left out for the birds. She says it isn't good for me, but I want to help clean it up.

Back home, I wag my tail impatiently, waiting for my water bowl to get filled. Only fresh water will do; any water there before my walk is unacceptable. Mom brings it in, and I stand in front of her, waiting expectantly.

"Fred, you gotta get out of the way. I need to put your water down." She sidesteps me to put it on the tray. Mom and Dad think I am a messy drinker and bought me a special drink mat.

67

This is the worst part of my day when Dad has already gone to work, and Mom is about to leave. I try to convince her to let me go with her; after all, I am a working dog, but she insists I stay home with my human. I love going places and am such a good boy, but Mom doesn't budge and leaves for work.

I hear the car leave and get onto my favorite spot on the couch—the big corner side with the Freddy indent in it. I curl up like a donut and sigh as I drift off for my first nap.

Throughout the day, my other human pets me, gives me treats, and lets me into the backyard. I love lying on the deck in the spring. It is my favorite time of the year. It is not too cold or too hot, and the sun feels perfect on my fur.

Once I've had enough deck time, I go back into the house and to my spot on the couch for another nap. Mom and Dad have been gone for years; I hope they didn't forget about me.

The noise of a car door wakes me. I listen, waiting to ensure it is who I think it is. It is! I rush towards the door and bark "Welcome home." Mom is almost in the house; she can hear me already. Her key turns in the door; she is finally home.

"Hi babies, I missed you too. Let me take my coat and shoes off, and then I will give you some pets and love."

I plod over to Mom and stand beside her legs. I want her to know that I missed her and that she should have just stayed home with me. My brother and sister try to get her attention, but I'm the oldest, so I should be first.

I sniff her to make sure she is okay from being gone for so long.

Now that Mom is home, it won't be long before Dad is home. I love it when Dad comes home because I can always convince him to give me cookies. Mom is much stricter and won't give me a cookie before dinner. No matter how big my eyes get, she doesn't budge. I even tried to send my brother and sister in to convince her, but they weren't very lucky either.

Another car door slams, this time, it must be Dad! We all start barking, and Mom tries to quiet us, but we are too excited.

Dad walks in and goes to our cupboard before taking off his coat and shoes. I have him trained well. He comes over and gives us our cookies. Satisfied, I plop onto the floor, wag my tail, and stare at Mom again. She knows what I want.

"Freddy, you still have 20 minutes before dinner time."

I don't understand what that means. I think Mom wants me to starve. It is hours before she finally picks up my dinner bowl. As she fills it, I sit up tall and anxiously wait. Finally, she puts my bowl down, and I get to eat—my other favorite part of the day.

It doesn't take me long to finish my food. My sister finishes her dinner, and I lick her bowl to ensure she doesn't miss anything. My brother gets mad if I try to help him with his dinner, so I don't bother.

Mom notices that I'm done and brings me fresh water. At least I trained her to fetch my water whenever I want it.

I find a new, comfortable spot to relax and digest my food. I listen to my brother yell at my sister because she has a bone that he wants. He is so silly because there is another bone on the ground, but he only wants the one she has. He almost takes it from her, but she grabs it and lays beside me. I hate it when they play around me while I am trying to relax.

"Zen, stop bugging your sister. Here, have a different bone." Mom tries to give Zen another bone; it looks the same, but Mom doesn't understand that it smells different.

Mom sits beside me, and I nudge her hand. She knows what time it is, which is another thing I trained her well in. "Okay, okay. Let me get Dad, and we will go for your W."

She thinks I don't know what that means, but I know it is walk time. I won't make it easy for her; I won't get up until she picks up my leash. She needs to remember who is in charge.

Once she is holding my leash, I stop to finish drinking my water. Then I finally let her put it on me.

Dad takes my brother's leash, and Mom takes my sister and me. We go for a walk, and I get to sniff around again. Mom and Dad chatter about something, but I don't understand. They love it when I take them for a walk; they have human alone time.

Once we get home, Dad knows I need another cookie, and Mom knows to refresh my water bowl.

As I finish drinking, Dad sits in my spot; I like sharing it with him at night. I lay beside him, using his legs as my pillow. He knows it is time to pet me and that he cannot move unless I let him. Sometimes, I lie with Mom because she brushes me and helps me stay handsome.

Once it gets late, it's time for 'last pee.' I don't listen when Mom says it because I need to make Dad get up. After I finish outside, I will decide where I want to sleep. If I always sleep in Mom's bed, she might think she is the boss, so I mix it up. Sometimes, I go to Mom's room, sometimes on the couch, and sometimes with my other human.

Tomorrow will be another hard day of taking care of Mom and Dad. They are so lucky to have me.

"When most of us talk to our dogs, we tend to forget they're not people." - Julia Glass

Georgie

CALL ME ITCHY, SCRATCHY, HAPPY BOY

By Lori Keesey

My name is Georgie, and I don't hate anyone or anything, including the mangy cat that once lived next door to me. Every time he'd venture onto our porch uninvited, I ended up with his fleas. It was a horrible experience. Their non-stop biting nearly drove me crazy. But now, looking back, I see the cat and the fleas as a blessing. If I hadn't gotten infested, I might have never been called Itchy, Scratchy, or Happy Boy.

It's the best nickname ever. For one, it was accurate. And two, Ty, my human, coined that little endearment the first time I came down with a bad case of the ruthless tiny vermin.

He'd been sitting on the couch, watching me, stretched out on the living room floor, gnawing and chewing, trying feverishly to rid myself of those little devils that had taken up residence beneath my brindled-colored fur. He smiled as he ran his fingers through his tousled, dirty-blond hair.

"What's the matter, itchy, scratchy, happy boy? Got fleas?" I'd stopped the nibbling and wag my tail.

The sound of his voice and the words flowing from his mouth made me happy, even though I didn't quite understand what they meant or what might happen next. "Well, you know what that means."

I did not. And I waited, my head resting on my front paws, as my eyes followed Ty getting up and walking a few paces to the hallway bathroom, a tiny room nestled between two smallish bedrooms. I heard the rummaging and the slammed cabinet door. The muttering when a bottle dropped in the bathtub before the shower turned on.

Uh-oh. What to do? What to do? Even to this day, I avoid getting wet, especially if it involves getting lathered in a sickly-sweet potion that makes me want to roll in poo.

I did the only thing I could think to do. I jumped onto the sofa and burrowed beneath my favorite puffy comforter heaped among the throw pillows and other random blankets. Stupid. I know. Because I always gave myself away. I couldn't help myself.

"Is there a dog in there?"

Still buried, I couldn't see Ty but could smell him and hear his laugh. He was close.

"Is there a dog in there?" He repeated the question, this time a bit louder, and all my inhibitions melted like yellow snow on a warm winter day. How could I hide from Ty? My tail thumped, causing the blanket to move up and down. "I knew it," he shouted happily. "There is a dog in there. Itchy, Scratchy, Happy Boy, you're getting a shower."

And I could feel my tail thumping again.
But that happened a while ago. I haven't seen Ty in a long time.

How long? I'm not sure. Though I can count and know exactly how many treats to expect after supper, I don't understand days, months, or years. I know a lot of time has passed since seeing Ty, watching him as he put on those silly shorts he'd wear when he'd go to the river—a place I visited once but refused to enter.

My memories of him have begun to fade, but certain smells and sounds, even sights, will bring him back into focus, like the

74

sound of running water and the smell of shampoo. And that's when I miss him the most and start looking for him, waiting for him, and wondering why he left.

Ty wasn't my first human. I'd had two others before coming to him. And now, I have two more. A lot of humans have given me lots of experiences. And the lesson? Some humans don't deserve dogs like me.

That's why my heart missed a beat when Ty came to a place where strangers had caged me, among many other dogs. We whined and cried at night, wanting someone to love us and take us home. When I saw him coming amid the frenzied barks of my companions, my mouth stayed shut. I stood a little straighter, wanting to impress this man with the twinkling eyes and loud voice.

He crouched down to get a better look at me. "Hey, little buddy," he said, inserting his fingers through the metal bars to touch my face. He looked up at the other human, one of many who brought food every day.

"What's his name?"

"Georgie," the other said.

"I'll take him."

My heart hammered. My backside wiggled manically, put in motion by my wagging tail. He'd no more use me for target practice than kick me across the room. We could be buds, I figured, and my intuitions proved dead-on.

Twice a day, he'd loop a homemade leash around my neck and then drape the other looped end around his torso. He said it afforded hands-free walking, and off we went. What did I care? As I sniffed every bush on the route, he waited, staring at a little device he tucked away in his pocket before our adventure began.

Frick and Frack. Just the way I liked it, curled up in the dirty clothes hamper next to his desk or riding shotgun in his car, sniffing the awesomeness that wafted through the partially opened window as he sang at the top of his lungs.

And then poof. He disappeared.

I'm not complaining.

I now live with "Mom" and "Dad"—the names Ty called them when we stopped by to visit. It was the highlight of the week for me. The barking dogs in the distant valley. The rabbits and squirrels. Crazy smells that got my nostrils twitching until I found the source. I'd either roll in it or bring it home, making Ty laugh that big, head-turning guffaw when I dropped a leg bone, tendons and all, at his feet.

"Whatcha got there, Itchy, Scratchy, Happy Boy? I gotta get a picture of that."

I guess that's why I got so worried when he went missing. Why did Mom and Dad have that little device that he carried everywhere? Why didn't they answer it when it trilled and pinged before it went completely silent?

Why did so many people visit, their eyes filling when anyone mentioned Ty's name or saw me sitting in the front yard? My ears tuned for the distinctive sound of his car. In my mind's eye, I could see his head bobbing and his hands drumming in beat to the too-loud music.

Why wouldn't Ty come home?

Like I said, that happened a long time ago. I've lived on the ridge with Mom and Dad longer than anywhere else, including Ty's little house in the city. My face has whitened, and chasing animals holds little appeal. But I still have free rein. I come and go as I please.

I know where to go if I'm hungry and want a midday snack. I'll trot down the hill to visit another set of humans. Sometimes, they leave the front door open, an invitation to enter. Sometimes, I find the door closed, but that doesn't stop me from getting what I want. I whine until one of the humans swings the door wide open and gives me a treat.

And then I'll wander back home, knowing exactly what Dad will say. "Find anything good out there?" I wag my tail and rest my head on his lap. He rubs my ears and belly just like Ty used to do. "You're a good dog, Georgie boy. What would we do without you?"

I guess I don't know what I'd do without them either. I have the best life ever.

But how I wish I could hear Ty's big, booming voice and the name I loved so much. Itchy, Scratchy, Happy Boy. How I wish I could hear it just one more time.

"When I look into the eyes of an animal. I do not see an animal. I see a living being. I see a friend. I feel a soul." - A.D. Williams

Grace

GRACE'S SOLAR EXPERIENCE

By H. M. Rush

My wife and I are retired. Our children have grown and left the scene of their youthful indulgences and formidable years. It's just the two of us and our dog, Grace. Grace was rescued as a puppy with her sister and brother. When we met the litter, it was love at first sight with Grace. It has been over seven years since that day.

Knowing her heritage is essential to understanding her instincts. Finding her roots was important. She was genetically tested. Perhaps we know more about her heritage than the rumors and folklore of our own personal heritage.

She has an assortment of backgrounds, including Boxer, Beagle, Lab, and some other mysterious stuff. It gives her a unique personality. She has the snout of a beagle, the olfactory sense of a boxer, and the ears and eyes of the other mysterious stuff.

I believe being adopted as she was, she feels a certain kinship with us, and regardless of what genetics dictate, she thinks she is one of us. We think of her as our family.

During the pandemic, Grace became our closest and only friend. She never wore a mask. Heaven forbid she would observe the 6-foot distance rule.

We would take her for secluded walks in woodland areas and attempt to teach her about the natural world. Whenever we would point and say, "Look, Grace, a bird" or some other creature, she looked in the direction we pointed. Her ears were up, and her eyes were focused. She was ready for whatever caught our interest and to participate in the conversation. Grace will look at anything we point out to her. It seems she can understand English.

She may understand English better than others, including humans. In a way, one could argue that her mental abilities are stronger than mine. After all, my understanding of her language is negligible. Believe me, I have tried to understand and speak dog.

Occasionally, I will howl or let out a small bark, trying to relate. Grace gives me a strange look and walks away. My wife does the same, which further supports the idea that Grace is more intelligent than I am.

One day, while walking with my lovely wife and Grace (of course), she (my lovely wife) asked a question. "What will you do with Grace during the solar eclipse?" I was stunned. Why would such a question be asked? Is there an agenda to keep Grace from enjoying the eclipse with the family? Since when was Grace not a member of the family? Why would we do anything different?

Whatever the reasoning for this question, I firmly believe Grace needed her day in the sun. Her dignity as a family member was at stake. Our whole family, including Grace, will be in Erie for the totality event.

Not wanting a domestic incident, I explained in painful detail my well-thought-out plan to research the science and market for canine solar glasses. Once we find a pair, we order them on eBay or Amazon and teach Grace how to wear solar glasses. It should be a snap.

Grace appreciates learning new things and loves being part of the pack, so this is a win for her. The beauty of a long marriage is that a small amount of hearing loss is a good thing. I could not hear exactly what my lovely wife muttered, but I am sure she was in awe of my well-thought-out plan.

As with love and war, plans are always brilliant until enacted. I needed some expert advice. Who better to discuss my plan with than an eye doctor? So, I called my Optometrist and shared my concerns with him.

I He explained that being able to understand English, more or less, Grace will look up at the solar event every time someone says, "Look at that," and points to the sky. It will burn her little eyeballs out.

In his expert opinion, he concluded that a dog looking at the solar eclipse was a bad thing. He suggested Grace stay inside or not look at the sun. "Don't encourage it," he said. He did not seem to take this conversation seriously as one would expect from a doctor/patient relationship. But this did not deter me from the goal. Grace will enjoy the totality with the family.

As the optometrist discussion was useless, I needed to dive deeper into the research. Indeed, I needed to find more expert opinions. The wonder of the 21st century is the ease of obtaining information.

Any knowledge a person would want is floating around in this cloud of electrons called the internet. Somewhere in the great unknown, probably in a black box, these miraculous, magical electrons hold all the knowledge of humankind. All that is needed is a computer and some ideas for search words.

There are experts on anything and everything on the internet. My goal was to find the ones who think "outside the box" and supply canine solar glasses. The search on the internet was enlightening.

Strangely, most of the experts agreed with my Optometrist. It seemed evident that a conspiracy was afoot to prevent our "best friends" from enjoying this celestial event. However, not all hope is lost. There are sunglasses for dogs. These things are engineered for a dog's head. Unfortunately, none of the sunglasses available were ISO or NASA-approved for Canine Solar viewing. I needed a plan that was expert-proof.

Solar glasses work for humans; shouldn't they, if modified, work for dogs? ISO and NASA have approved these glasses. The initial attempt to fit Grace with a good pair of solar glasses proved a resounding failure. Her dog head just wasn't made for human eyewear. We had to do better.

Fortunately, there were plenty of examples of canine eyeglass-wear on the internet. With a handsome amount of free solar glasses on hand, Grace was fitted with many iterations of redesigned glasses.

A remarkable aspect of Grace's personality is her love of capitalism. If you wish her to do something, pay her. She accepts doggie biscuits, cheese, hotdogs, and any other quickly redeemable reward.

These incentives piqued Grace's interest in the project, and a successful outcome was at hand. It took a lot of trial and error to engineer glasses that fit her. Grace appreciated the high volume of rewards.

With the miracle of modern engineering and the internet, Grace had her ISO/NASA-approved solar eyewear ready to enjoy totality with the pack. The family was excited. There was one slight challenge: The glasses were so dark that Grace could not see anything. She just sat with her glasses firmly on her snout.

The day of totality arrived. The family was stationed in the yard. Some were praying for the clouds to part, hoping that Moses was listening, and others were cursing Mother Nature for allowing clouds to appear on this day of total eclipse.

Grace sat with her fitted designer solar eyeglasses. As we were entranced with the mooning of the sun, Grace removed her glasses, retrieved a frisbee, and dropped it on my lap. In her universe, perhaps a flying disc is a celestial event.

As long as her pack was together and enjoying the moment with her, she had her own lifetime event. She enjoys it daily.

"When you look into the eyes of an animal you've rescued. you can't help but fall in love."

Paul Shaffer

Kimberly

I AM SHE

By Andrea Hochgatterer

1998, we set out to pick up a puppy on a chilly mid-April morning.

"Ah, I am not sure about having a dog." I asked my husband, "Are you sure it's a good idea?"

"Trust me, you'll see."

Never having owned a pet before, I felt slightly uneasy and uncertain of what to expect.

I hadn't seen the dog before, as my husband had chosen her on a whim when he spotted a roadside sign reading, "Black Shepard for sale." Having listened to his enthusiasm for several days, I finally relented.

"Ok, I give in; let's give it a try."

Yes, there, I have said it. It was an "It" to me, just a dog, so when I first met that tiny yapping creature, who decided in her excitement to wee straight onto my new coat, I was not impressed at all.

However, watching her an hour later marching into our house, tiny tail wagging in the air, completing her rounds of inspection full of confidence, finally deciding our abode was fit for "Her Royal Highness" and plonking herself down in front of the open fire, she did impress me. No anxiety, no whimpering or yapping now that she had made her decision. "My house!"

So, let me properly introduce Kimberly, our Black German Shepherd (8.3.1998 - 8.3.2011), who won our hearts, made us laugh and taught us animal communication at its best. She left a massive mark on all our lives, including urban foxes, whom she joined for nightly walkabouts, our children, and most of all, our cats. Plus, she saved the inevitable mice, birds, and frogs from our feline family members' clutches (or rather claws).

"Boring!"

One hot, sunny summer morning, a few months after Kim's arrival, I was working diligently at my desk. By now, the familiar huffing and puffing was coming from underneath my chair.

"Come on, Kim, I wish I had your life, curled up underneath my owner's chair, lazing my life away; what an easy dog's life you have."

"Phhh," comes her response. Her strange hazel eyes stare at me, making clear the suffering she must bear living with me. She conveniently forgets all the chicken soups I cooked when she is feeling poorly.

"I am bored, Mum!"

"Okay, here's what we'll do: five more minutes, and then we'll play."

Five minutes later, "Woof, it's time now!" comes the Royal command, "Let's play chasers!"

They took turns chasing each other around the table, over settees, into the garden, and up and down the stairs; what fun, what a racket! Until she suddenly disappears.

"Hey Kim, where are you?"

Searching high and low, I did not find her until, "Ta-da!" She suddenly jumped out at me from behind the bathroom door, giving me the shock of my life.

"Gotcha!" she grins at me.

"Oh, you tricky beastie!"

Surrogate cat mum

We did not anticipate how fiercely protective Kim would be.

As the oldest of her litter and having been born in a horse box of large stables, she had quickly learned from her Mum's behavior that any outsider was to be kept at bay to ensure the survival of the litter.

Neighbors were barked at, visitors discouraged, and however tiny and unthreatening she looked to us, people were afraid of her.

Something had to be done. Puppy training wasn't available, so we regularly took Kim to the nearby pet shop to socialize with people and maybe find some animal friends, too.

Bingo! She met a new friend! There was a minute Tortoiseshell kitten, which Kim took on as her own, quickly followed by Spike Milligan and then MacMac (ref. Mac the Knife, as he turned out to be the biggest closed-door and window cracker in town).

Kim's cats slept on her belly and were allowed to whack her ears while she slept. She'd protect her brood when a catfight was kicking off outside. Yet, they were never allowed to take a sneaky bite from her food. They were picked up by the scruff of their necks, carried to their food station, and unceremoniously dumped into their food. As they managed to scramble free, she would reach between their back legs, flicking them back in.

"There you go, that'll teach you!"

"Such fun to send people flying too."

She did not stop with the cats, though. Once she discovered the same was possible with humans—not that we ever tried to steal

89

her food, of course—she'd catch me unaware and send me flying many times.

The same goes for the dog walker, who had laughed me off to her own detriment when I warned her about Kim's new-found fun and games until she returned covered in mud one day. She had gone flying, too, a victim of Kim's pranks.

"I am royalty."

I am sure you know dogs who carry their leash, are keen to carry their owner's newspaper, or even pick up freshly delivered letters.

Not so Kim: "Phhh, who do you think I am? You pick it up if you want; I am not a fetch-and-carry kind of dog."

Ok, that put us straight. Clearly, being royal, she was much more a catch than a fetch kind of dog.

"I can catch a tuppence piece."

"Easy, try me! Now, from further back! Yeah! Now further!"

She could catch a tuppence piece, wide-mouthed, then spit it out for us to retrieve, of course. Eventually, we upped the game using a tiny one-penny piece, and she again successfully royal-goalie catches all, until one day, she suddenly looks crestfallen, "Oh no! What happened to the penny? You haven't swallowed it, have you? Or you lost it; let's go and look."

We'd search, leaving no stone unturned, sofas lifted, rugs shaken, and no penny found. "Are you sure you haven't swallowed it?"

With a big grin (dogs grin, they do), she slowly opens her mouth, her long tongue protruding. There is the penny!

"Cheeky!"

"You promised!"

A balmy summer evening, hubby back from work, we laze away in the garden, watching the sun go down. "What's up with Kim?" asks hubby.

"I don't know, why?"

"She has avoided my eye, sniffed around the garden, and ignored us for the last half hour."

"Oh no, I forgot! I promised her a bath!"

Earlier in the day, I had run myself a bubble bath with added Lavender oil, one of Kim's favorites. She could munch herself through sways of early lavender, chewing a few bumbles on the way (one thing we could never stop her from doing), so picking up the scent of lavender, she is ready to jump in.

"Nooo, Kim, don't take my face towel soaked in the bath water; when Dad gets home, you can have your bath, ok?"

Snatching the towel from my hand, "Harrumph," she slinks off, her lady dog bottom swaying in her funny signature gait.

So, I ask Her Royal Highness, "Does Kimmie want a bath?"

Wow, change of attitude! The excitement of a full-grown Shepard dog!

A bath with bubbles and lavender drenches the whole bathroom, including ourselves, until eventually, we watch a happy Kim "running it off" in the low evening sun.

"What a strange dog we've got."

"Well, you chose her," I say as I wink at hubby.

"No wool to be pulled over MY eyes!"

Kim hated those shops that sold dog chews and bones. While politely accepting the goodies, she would sneak into the garden and casually bury them. I discovered a huge bone deep beneath the old lilac bush one day. Intending to have fun, I secretly retrieved it, washed off the dirt, and wrapped it in paper (she loved unwrapping presents).

"Look, Kim, here is a present for you."

Excitedly, she starts pulling off the wrapper, but then, "Hey, what's that?" she stops short, "I know that one!" And with that, she saunters off, digs the exact spot where I discovered the bone in the first place, and picks up the bone to re-bury it in its rightful place without deigning me a look.

When Kim inevitably passed, we were grief-stricken, including the cats. In particular, a later addition, Monty Python. He had the cheekiest grin and wildest mop of ginger hair you have ever seen and would sit in Kim's favorite spot looking at me accusingly, "What have you done with my Kim?"

Inconsolable, he one day packed his bags, so to speak, and moved somewhere across the green. Sometimes, I could spot him running past our back door, avoiding my gaze. (An important reminder: animals grieve, too.)

Everyone loved Kim, and she loved us. She was part of our family in a way I never thought possible. She taught us many things: play, have fun, care for loved ones, listen, communicate, and treat your animals as beloved fellow creatures.

A truly blessed life.

"Shelter dogs aren't broken. They've simply experienced more life than other dogs. Don't pity a shelter dog. Adopt one and be proud to have their greatness by your side." - Anonymous

Kringle

KRISTMAS KRINGLE

By Joseph Dolak

My name is Kringle, and this is my story. The first six years of my life were not the best. You see, I came from a hoarding situation where I spent the first six years of my life in a terrible place. But the nice people at The ANNA Shelter came to my rescue.

My group was known as The Rescue 51 Group, as there were 51 of us who received a new lease on life. After The Anna Shelter fixed us up and got us healthy, they had an adoption day at our local pet store. We were in our cages, and this nice man walked by my cage with another dog on a leash. He looked at me, and I stared into his eyes; I began to wag my long tail at him; mind you, I only weighed 18lbs, so my whole body was moving with my tail wagging.

He asked the attendant if he could see me in the play area to see if his dog and I got along with each other. We were in the room, and this is where the magic started. I immediately jumped up on his lap and stared into his eyes. I knew I could get to his heart, so I sprawled out on his lap and started to lick his hand. I knew I had him by his reaction, so my next step was to convince the other dog.

I got down on the floor and walked near the other dog, who was way bigger than me, but we were good with each other; he was older and didn't seem to mind me.

What happened next was the start of the best day of the rest of my life. The man said to the attendant, "I will take Kringle." My tail never moved so fast. I think it was ready to fall off. I was so happy to go home with this man and his dog because I knew he would care for me and give me a new and better life.

Before we left, we had to take a going-home picture for the Anna Shelter people; they were so lovely to me. So, from that December day at the pet store, I walked out as Kringle, which the staff named me. My new Dad loved my name and let it stay.

When we arrived at my new home, which was nice, I got to run around and do all the sniffing I wanted to with my new big brother. He nipped at me a few times, but that was me getting a little too close because I was free to move around. I had to stay in my kennel at night, so I didn't pester my big brother.

The next day, I met my dad's son Bryce, who was starting college and was living with us. We became "Besties." I was his study buddy. I would lay by his feet as he did his homework. My big brother, Casper, would hang out with my dad sometimes, but he liked being by himself mostly.

As the days went by, I got more comfortable being in the house, and when I went outside to potty, I saw this cold white stuff on the ground. This was something new to me, and I was not a fan of it. It was cold on my paws. Not good, but I did get used to it.

A few weeks later, Dad and Bryce brought home this big tree and put it up in the corner of the room, and I thought, "Look at that big pee spot," but Dad let me know right away when I tried to squat next to it that was not what it was for.

As the months and years went by, I was having the time of my life until my big brother became very sick, and my dad had tears in his eyes. I crawled up onto his lap and heard him say, "It's just you and me now, Kringle," as Casper had passed away.

I was the only one now. I often looked for my big brother but could not find him. I was so lost for a few months; I was now alone when my dad and Bryce were off to work and school. I was confused at first, but as time went on, I was able to adjust, and Dad gave me the run of the house, which I enjoyed every minute of.

I loved being on the couch, which was so soft. I would curl up in my "C" position to get comfortable. I was living the life of a pampered pet. As I became more and more comfortable being the only pup in the house, I began to find new places to hide until Dad and Bryce came home for the night.

As soon as I heard them open the door, I would come out of the bedroom from one of my hiding spots behind the bed and casually walk out to greet them. My Dad loved his recliner, so I would jump onto his chest and fall asleep together; that was the best.

My next best place was my dad's bed, which was a warm waterbed. Sleeping beside my dad made me so happy and warm on those cold, wintery days and nights.

As I got older, now 11 years old, my eyesight started to get bad. I had cataracts, which made me bump into things, but I knew my way around well enough. My dad always took me in for checkups at the vet. Then, one day, the Vet found a mass inside me and told my dad that it wasn't good.

It progressed quickly, and I became very sick. My dad gave me medicine to help me with the pain, but this was a battle that I couldn't overcome. I remember my dad lying next to me, saying, "It's ok, Kringle, I understand if you have to leave me. I don't want you to suffer." I could feel his hand on me as I closed my eyes. As I watched my dad walk away for the last time, I knew it was going to be hard for my dad and Bryce, but I wanted them to know they gave me the best life ever after they rescued me.

I will miss them very much. I know their hearts are broken now, but I want them to know I lived the best life ever with them. I appreciate them so much for the love they both gave me.

It was my time to cross the Rainbow Bridge and run free of pain, but I will look back, waiting to see them again one day. I am running, playing, and pain-free with my big brother Casper.

My name is Kringle. Thank you for letting my Dad share my story with you.

"Most people say if I was rich. I'd buy designer clothes and diamonds. I'm thinking I'd buy a sanctuary and rescue more animals." - Anonymous

Martin

UNWANTED, TURNED POPULAR THERAPY DOG

By Sue Anderson

Here I am in the later years of life, and I have had dogs for as long as I can remember. I could never imagine not having one or more four-legged canine buddies living in my home, creating a constant obstacle of stepping over them when they are sleeping in the middle of any floor in the house or wiping up muddy footprints on the kitchen floor when they come in from running outside in the mud. I was never particular about a breed, color, size, etc. So, I have had quite a variety of dog breeds over the years.

Collies had always been my favorite. I was introduced to them at age seven by my aunt and uncle, who had owned several collies. Starting at age 14, I also owned a collie, miniature poodles, a Shih Tzu, a Lhasa Apso, and several other breeds. I would lean toward a smaller dog to live with one of my collies.

Little did I know my pattern of mostly registered dogs would change and have an overwhelming effect on the rest of my life.

The story begins several years ago when a friend asked me to accompany her to a nearby town to rescue three 8-week-old puppies from an individual who had destroyed two puppies from a previous litter when he was unable to find a home for them. I explained that I would help with the rescue mission but did not want another dog when I was already the owner of three other dogs at the time.

Off we went on a road trip that would change the rest of my life. We returned with three 8-week-old puppies. We talked a mutual friend into taking one of the puppies, and we started searching to find two other unsuspecting future dog owners. The two puppies

101

were sort of cute. Each resembled the color of a "Rottie," the usual black and tan.

For the next few days, I decided to name these two orphans Martin and Luther until we could find homes for both. After placing ads in several vet offices and making phone calls to anyone I thought might want a puppy, we finally found a home for one of the puppies. The one named Luther.

After another week had passed, I was still Martin's foster parent. He was really rather cute and seemed to fit into the present "pack," but adding a fourth dog was out of the question. I decided to take him to the local shelter later in the week since no one I knew wanted a dog at that time.

Arrangements were made at the shelter to drop him off the following week. Martin stayed at my house, waiting for the transfer to occur. Martin must have known I was a real pushover for puppies. Two days later, he had successfully pushed his way into my heart.

I decided I couldn't possibly get rid of this puppy. I reluctantly added him to the three-dog pack, which was already living in my home. I kept telling myself that if someone stopped at the house, I could certainly explain that Martin was staying until I could find him a more permanent home.

Days turned into weeks, and Martin was still at my house, moving quite successfully into my heart. Since I have always been a strong believer in dog obedience training (necessary, of course, for the owner to be trained), I enrolled Martin in the puppy class for basic obedience and socializing with other puppies.

Even though I was told his ancestry was a combination of a Black Lab, Rottie, and a Border Collie, he also had very short legs for whatever reason. He was immediately nicknamed by the instructor "The Stump." He soared right through obedience class with flying colors. When asked about his breed, I started referring to him as a "summa."

Someone asked what a Summa is since they had never seen that breed listed with the AKC. I would laugh and explain he is a "summa," the sum of this and the sum of that. Little did I know this "Summa," the "Heinz 57" mutt, was destined for greater things.

It soon became clear that Martin had a unique personality and was natural at making friends with everyone he met. When we entered the second stage of training, he was a constant source of enjoyment for everyone who met him.

During one of the obedience classes, one of the therapy dog evaluators asked if I would be interested in Martin becoming a visiting therapy dog. She felt Martin had a great disposition with people, was friendly, and was low-keyed with his big, beautiful brown eyes.

Training Martin was such an easy task. He wasn't "treat" oriented during training, but he certainly was thrilled with all the love being bestowed on him by everyone and loved the "kiss" on his forehead every time he completed the required tasks in training.

After the second training session, I decided to try this therapy dog stuff and signed up for Martin to start the therapy dog certification process.

He met the basic requirements to be a therapy dog certification candidate. He was over one year old, friendly, and good with both people and other dogs. He loved attention and was attentive to most new activities. We started the required visits to the local nursing homes in the spring of that year, and a few months later, Martin was declared an official therapy dog. We immediately started regular visits to some of the local nursing homes.

When the local cancer treatment center opened, the director was looking for any dogs that could be involved at the cancer treatment center. Martin's veterinarian mentioned the offer at the cancer center to me and thought Martin could be a perfect candidate.

The dogs would be there to comfort and support the patients when they were receiving chemotherapy or radiation treatment. Martin worked at the cancer center two to three days each week, sharing his gentle demeanor with everyone who entered the facility.

He worked at the cancer center for over 14 years, providing comfort to the patients and staff. Everyone knew "Martin" and waited patiently while he made his rounds with the patients each working day. Martin did his job perfectly during daytime visits to the cancer center and the local hospital.

When he wasn't working at the cancer center, he could be found working at other community facilities. An elementary school heard about Martin and asked if he could visit with the special needs students. While wearing his therapy dog tag, he became an attentive, kind, loving visitor day after day in the community.

He spent his days at home chasing cats and barking at the cows in the pasture beside my house. His favorite pastime was waiting for an occasional groundhog to cross into his domain. Within a few minutes, he would chase down the critter and deposit the remains in the corner of the field. Or we would go down to one of the ponds on the property to cool down and rest in the sun.

From an unwanted dog only days from becoming a resident at the local shelter, he became a community favorite therapy dog. When the cancer center had its summer celebration of recovery, past patients always stopped at the therapy dog booth to see Martin and share with others how important he had been to their journey through cancer treatment.

As time passed, Martin must have told the other dogs in the household pack how much he loved therapy dogs and how they needed to do the same thing.

Martin will always be "Number One," but since then, the dog family has grown quite a bit, and the one thing they all had in common was serving as local therapy dogs.

A shitzu, a Lhasa Apso, and three collies have joined the ranks as official therapy dogs certified through the Alliance of Therapy Dogs in Cheyenne, Wyoming.

Each one has been memorable to the many clients in the cancer center and other community facilities, as they shared their love and gentle spirit with schoolchildren, nursing home residents, special needs kids, and anyone they have ever met.

Martin was the total joy of my life for 15 wonderful years. His notoriety became his constant wagging tail and his big brown eyes. In the past twenty-three years since Martin started his work as a therapy dog, I have seen firsthand the importance of pet therapy visits for the local nursing homes, schools, libraries, and special facilities in the area.

The therapy dog group continues to willingly share their time in various situations. With long hours of loneliness and isolation for many of the patients in the local nursing homes, dog visits provide an opportunity for a special kind of contact and often a calming influence for the person.

Many patients share their stories and pictures of past pets in their lives. As Martin and the other therapy dogs move from room to room at the nursing homes, the dogs patiently stand and wait for residents to have contact with the dogs in our group.

Through his memory, Martin's spirit has continued to let a multitude of other therapy dogs in the community share his kindness and gentle disposition.

Working with the other pet owners and their dogs has become a rewarding experience for everyone involved with the therapy dog program. Martin passed away almost eight years ago, but his memory remains with me every day, every time I share my other dogs in therapy dog work.

Therapy dogs can range from purebred to show dogs to classic mutts like Martin. Size doesn't matter, from a 150-pound Newfoundland to a 5-pound Japanese Chen. The criteria are simple: have a well-trained dog and a dog owner who wants to share his or her dog with others. If interested, remember Martin's story and join a therapy dog group in your community.

"Adopting a shelter dog is an excellent way to turn love into action. The love you receive is an extraordinary extra benefit."

Abby Underdog

Nemo

NEMO'S DEBUT

By Marybeth Haines

Quote: *"Dogs are the most amazing creatures; they give unconditional love. For me, they are the role model for being alive."* – Gilda Radner (comedian)

Hi friends, my name is Nemo, and I'm a Chihuahua living in St. Catharines, Ontario, Canada. It's really nice to meet you!

My mom talks with animals and told me she was writing a chapter for this book. My ears perked right up when I heard this, and I wanted to be included. So, I gave my mom an energetic nudge, and she heard me!

She told me this could be my chapter, and I could write whatever I wanted. I'm so happy about this!

So, with my mom's help in translating my words, I want to share something about animals and how we come to help you, the humans we love so much. I'd like to be your teacher and share my perspective.

Introduction
We, as animals, come into your life for a purpose and a reason, and we come here to fulfill this in many ways.

Some animals experience traumatic events, others have physical or medical issues, and some have positive life experiences. Just like humans, we come here to live our lives learning, growing, and healing. Thank you for helping us with this.

Keeping all the above in mind, I'd like to share with you some deeper meanings of an animal's role in your life.

Mirroring
Animals are teachers, and we come to teach the humans we share life with. We teach in many ways. Just as you might look in a mirror to witness the reflection of what's happening in your life, we might mirror that same thing back to you with our behavior.

Have you ever had an animal drive you crazy with a behavior? I mean, really crazy, where it bothered you so much? I invite you to reflect on that time and ask if what was being mirrored to you was something you were working on deep within yourself.

With the mirror analogy, I can explain this further to help you see from an 'outside of you' perspective, the mirror of what's happening 'inside of you.' Sometimes you see it, sometimes you don't.

That's what mirroring is all about, and it will continue to show up for you until you are ready to work through the learning. As animal teachers, we are patient as we help you with this aspect.

Soul Connection
Our souls are connected, and it's part of the journey to go through these things together. Through this connection, we can show you these things and remind you there is always a solution to every situation. For humans open to receiving these teachings, huge shifts can be had.

Remembering that we are together with you for a reason and that there is a soul's purpose to our time together is a clue here to realize. We are together with you for a purpose, and you are with us for a purpose, too. Together, on a soul level, we can learn from each other in many ways.

Healing

As animals, we possess healing capabilities. When we live our lives as animals, we come without ego or judgment and journey through various life experiences. There's a lot that we are here to learn.

Sometimes, we can heal through our touch. Other times, it's through how we look at you with our eyes. A lot of times, we heal by just being our genuine selves, and we don't have to try because healing energy is just emitted from us naturally. We are here to help, and we are here to heal. Not all animals are here to be healers, but all animals have the ability to heal.

Adaptors

A few years ago, I remember my mom buying a laptop—a MacBook, she calls it. It has special plugs on the sides, and most of the things she needs to plug into it only have standard cords. She would get frustrated because her regular cord wouldn't fit into the specialized hole, so she would always ask my dad for help.

Dad helped her buy a custom adaptor for her computer so that she could plug in these things and have them fit and work. (Dad is the tech guy in our family…. Mom, not so much!! Ha ha!)

For example, when Mom plugs in her webcam now, she uses her special gadget to ensure the plug fits. She needed a tool to help her do this, and that tool is what I call an 'adaptor.'

What I'd like to share with you about this analogy is that when humans go through life, sometimes you have a hard time making things fit into their 'plugs' or 'sockets.' Sometimes, they don't fit because they're not the right plug, and you need an adaptor to help get the right fit.

Animals have come forward in this same way to help you adapt, heal, and work through certain situations, challenges, and life experiences.

Animals are also here as 'adaptors' to help you find the right fit so that you can experience what you have come here to learn with ease and with beautiful healing support…from us!

We bring the right adaptor that is unique to your situation and help you bridge the gap between the two sides to make it whole.

Our Time Together
An animal's life isn't as long as a human's. Chances are, if a human has an animal in their life, they will also experience the death of that animal. This can be very hard for that human.

One reason we are often predecessors to humans is that we can bring love through transition. The way we share time together is a gift, and when the time comes for our passing, we feel the call back to our spiritual home with our creator/source.

We are not on earth for a long time compared to humans; we are there for the right and destined time as our soul contracts play out.

There is a reason our lives aren't as long as humans, and we are meant to be predecessors to many humans because of the gifts we bring them and the gifts we receive from them.

We come for a reason, a time period, and we leave with gifts that will remain even after our physical existence on Earth is completed.

The experience of our passing can be hard. We don't like to leave our humans with the emotions that we, on a physical level,

112

have left them with. On a soul's level, however, we know that there is learning our humans need to receive from our time together.

The Gifts We Share

One thing I know for sure is the gifts we, as animals, bring to our humans always remain with them, even after we've transitioned to spirit. Our physical presence may no longer exist, but the gifts and memories we shared remain forever.

Another thing to remember is that we are still the essence of who we were on earth, although our form may have changed from physical to energetic. Always know we are still very much a part of your life, which will never change.

This is something that humans are here to learn, which is why I wanted to share this as one of the many ways we, as animals, are here to help. Often, the loss experienced from our death is felt deeply, but our transition back to spirit serves a purpose.

Even after we leave our physical bodies, we still guide our humans from spirit, which is a gift I wish to remind you all about. Your animals are still with you, embracing you with love.

As I finish this chapter, my name is Nemo, and I've come to Earth as a teacher and a healer as part of my soul's journey.

I hope my guidance serves a purpose as you learn how the animals in your life have come to help you. There is a reason why you found each other, and the gifts they have come to give are endless!

Thank you for reading this. I'm so happy to have shared this with you! I'm now a published author! Yahoo!

Love Nemo the Chihuahua - Teacher and Healer

"Unconditional love is as close as your nearest shelter." - Anonymous

Pepper

A NEED TO MOVE FORWARD

By Reva Wheeler

Pepper is an intelligent and agile Norwegian elkhound and miniature Australian shepherd Mix. She is energetic, quickly learns new things, and is eager to please.

On Wednesday, she loves the opportunity to show off her skills in Agility class. When at home, she is usually perched in front of her favorite picture window, relaxing in her safe zone, or she is on watch waiting for the opportunity to alert her household that something is not right outside,

I met Pepper at the Anna shelter in November 2022. The shelter had several dogs in a foster-to-adopt situation due to an abuse/neglect case in Erie, PA.

The story that was on the news was heartbreaking. I've never fostered a dog, so this was new for our family. Pepper's name at the shelter was Louise. She was there with her sister Thelma, and it was difficult to tell them apart; they were almost identical twins.

When she entered the little meeting area, she put on quite a show for us, doing circles, chasing her tail, and offering tons of kisses. She was eight months old, only thirty-two pounds, and thin for her size.

Her black coat was uniquely marked with tan mixed in, and her eyes were marked with beautiful tan circles. Her ears stood straight up, and she had a poofy, curly tail that would have brought anyone a smile, especially when she shook it in excitement.

One of the workers at the shelter popped by to see how our visit was going. She asked what we thought, and when she asked, Pepper got up and placed herself between Dan and me; she politely sat down and looked up at the staff as if to say, yes, I will take them; these are my people. We felt the same way. Pepper was on her way to start a new life and a new adventure.

There were many obstacles that she needed to overcome due to spending the first eight months of her life with limited contact with people and not receiving proper care and nutrition.

We discovered she had a severe case of a resistant hookworm that took several months of treatment before she was worm-free. She feared everything would shut down and freeze at times. Pepper had to learn how to go up and down stairs, play with toys, walk on a leash, sniff the ground when she was outside, and that our basement was not the proper place to potty.

She found a safe zone on our living room couch, where she went when she first arrived at our home. The first month, she tried to blend in with the sofa cover. We had a rule in the house that if she was in her safe zone, no one was to bother her. Eventually, she came out of her shell and started perching on the couch, looking out a large picture window. This allowed her to see the world outside without the stress of being in it.

We started obedience class right away. She needed to build confidence, and I needed to learn how to communicate with her better.

In our first class, she discovered she could bark, and that is what she did. She would bark so loud you could not hear the teacher.

117

A few of the most important lessons I learned in class were that you need to be more exciting than everything else in the room to get your dog's attention and that it is important to bond with your dog through play.

After two obedience courses, I wanted to explore agility to see if it would fit Pepper well. She appeared to do well and picked up on learning jumps, tunnels, and teeters very quickly.

Pepper can be highly focused and follow my cues on the course perfectly. I am overly proud of what we can accomplish when working as a team. We also have days when we struggle on the field. She may be more interested in the dogs on the side of the fence, or she wants to show off her independent side by running the course by herself, without me.

Unbelievably, at times, she almost nails exactly what we were instructed to do; it is like she heard the teacher and decides okay, I will take care of this and off she goes.

In August 2023, we received the news that pepper was a permanent part of our family. I remember calling everyone and sending texts with the news. I do not know if she realized what was happening that day, but it seemed like she had a positive shift in her bonding with the family.

I believe she sensed I was more at ease, which came from knowing she did not have to return to her previous environment.

Pepper is my friend and my teammate. On days I may be working longer or spending too much time on my cell phone, she will politely approach me and lay her head on my lap.

She is a positive distraction from my hectic work life. Thanks to Pepper, I spend more time outside enjoying the world around me. She makes me laugh when we play tug or work with the flirt pole, or she tries a sly move to grab her toy rabbit.

She is always ready to greet me when I come home, wagging her tail so hard her whole body moves, telling me how happy she is to see me. She warms my heart when she is lying down, letting out a sigh and a small, content moan. I know she feels this is her home, her safe zone.

We have been going to Something Els Dog School, LLC, for a year. Our teacher has been wonderful, and we are grateful for the team members in our class. Everyone has been patient, understanding, and willing to help us work through some of Pepper's behaviors.

Recently, Pepper started to display increased reactivity to people and other dogs. One Wednesday evening, we had a terrible night at class; Pepper ran circles on the field and barked, ignoring anyone trying to reign her in.

On my way home, I was thinking about everything I was doing with training, trying to pinpoint what I was doing wrong and why she was behaving like this. That weekend, I finally started to understand what Pepper had been trying to tell me.

I was determined to walk with Pepper at Pleasant Ridge Park, a local park in my area. My daughter came along to enjoy the trails. Usually, there are not many people when we go, making it an ideal location for us.

This Saturday, several families with children and pets were present. I was concerned about how Pepper would react once she got out of the car. We have encountered many people who do not understand what Pepper is going through when she acts this way, and sometimes, there are comments like, "You need to get some training for that dog."

I paused, took a deep breath, and started the walk. As soon as Pepper saw some people, she lunged and barked. I tried to distract her and regain her focus but was unsuccessful, so we moved forward.

The more we moved forward, the calmer she became when seeing people, and she was more focused on me. We had such a wonderful walk; Pepper was becoming playful, running through mud and then back to me; you could see how happy she was.

That evening, I realized she had been trying to tell me what she needed from me. I need to be calm and keep us moving forward, allowing her to work through her bouts of reactivity and to watch for her cues telling me she is good or when it may be time to take a break.

In March 2024, Pepper will be turning two. Thank you, Anna Shelter, for your commitment to rescuing animals in need and for allowing me to care for Pepper. They say things occur in one's life for a reason, and I believe that.

Pepper needed nurturing, a family, and a home. I needed a friend. Pepper has accomplished so much since November 2022, and now that she is a permanent part of our family, we will work together to get through any obstacle that may come our way.

"Once you have had a wonderful dog, a life without one is a life diminished." - Dean Koontz

Scrappy

THE SWEETEST BLESSING

By Cheryl Pepicello

The year was 2019. A message on social media asked for donations of a specific brand of dog food for a dog that was reported left at a dumpster and rescued by The Erie Humane Society.

I immediately felt compelled to purchase this specific dog food brand and take it to The Humane Society.

After dropping off food donations several times, Officer Lisa, who rescued this dog, invited me to meet the little guy. She took me to her office and opened the door. I saw the tiniest fur baby. He lacked most of his fur, had no teeth, and had the sweetest face. He weighed only five pounds.

Meet Scrappy, the long-haired Chihuahua.

I picked up this little man and held his tiny body close as Officer Lisa shared his story.

This was not the first time he had been rescued. Before this, he had been found walking down a street alone.

For most of Scrappy's life, he lived in a crate and was used for breeding. He never walked with his owner or learned to play with toys or other dogs.

His days and nights were spent inside the crate, most likely alone or left with a female dog to enhance his owner's financial gains.

There was no bond, no connection. To them, he was just a pup for a purpose—not what I would call a good purpose. There was no love, care, compassion, or guilt for how they treated this helpless pup.

Since Scrappy would be further stressed by being put in a kennel at the shelter, Officer Lisa kept him in her office. He had a bed on her desk, next to her computer, where he would place his paw on her hand so she would pet him while she was typing her reports.

You see, he just wanted and needed a little bit of love and attention from someone who cared and saw him. If Officer Lisa stopped petting him, even for a moment, he would gently place his paw back on her hand as if to say, "Please love me."

Shortly after I met Scrappy, I brought my husband to meet him while we dropped off more food for him. When Tony picked up little Scrappy, he immediately placed his little head under my husband's chin and rested it on his heart. At that very moment, life was good for Scrappy and us.

It had been two and a half years since we lost our first fur baby, Rusty, after sixteen and a half years. We never thought we could open our hearts again because of the hard goodbye. Our hearts felt like they were broken into a million pieces when he passed away.

Scrappy opened our hearts, and we fell in love with him. We applied to adopt him and were elated to be chosen as his "fur-ever" family on May 8, 2019.

Scrappy brought such joy to our lives. He loved to go for walks on his leash, take car rides, and just be outdoors. On any given day, you would find him lying by a window or a door while the sun was shining in on him. His favorite pastime was lying on our deck alongside me, basking in the sun or cooling off in the shade.

Scrappy was a true lap dog. He would park himself on my lap and enjoy being brushed or napping there.

A favorite treat of his was plain Greek yogurt. He would do circles when he saw he was about to get a spoonful. This was the only treat his belly could tolerate.

On our day trips, people would always approach us and ask about this sweet little boy.

He loved to sit by the water and watch the waves, seagulls, and boats. He loved going on adventures around Erie with my sister and brother-in-law.

They would take him to festivals and have sleepovers when we were out of town.

There were days my husband took him to work so he would not be home alone all day if I was going to be gone for any length of time. Scrappy would curl up in his donut bed on the desk, and my husband would pet his boy while working, just like Officer Lisa. So much love, so many snuggles.

Every morning, we had to wake Scrappy up. He enjoyed sleeping in our bed and would stay there all day if he could.

Every night, religiously, at 8:00 PM, he would jump off my lap and turn to look at me. He stared into my eyes, announcing it was time to go to bed. If I did not immediately leave the couch to join him, he would walk to the doorway leading to our bedroom and turn to me again as if to say, "It's time to turn in, Mom; let's go."

Of course, I obliged, even if it meant lying there, unable to fall asleep quite yet. It gave me time to reflect and, more importantly, meant more snuggles with my boy. How lucky am I?

Fast forward to October 2023. Scrappy no longer wanted his favorite treat, Greek yogurt. He had no interest in food. A call to the vet was in order, and an appointment with bloodwork revealed that he had elevated kidney levels. They hospitalized him and, for 48 hours, tried flushing and rehydrating him. His little body could not fight, so we had to make the unbearable decision to say goodbye.

We took him home for one more night of snuggles and to let our family say goodbye.

Upon arrival at the vet that next day, I knew in my heart our lives were forever changed both by his presence and his passing. I held him in my arms as he took his last breath, crossing the rainbow bridge. Just like that, he was gone.

I am forever grateful for the time we had together and all the memories we made. I am still wrapping my head around his passing. I still expect to see him when I walk through the door at home.

To some, he may have been just a dog. To me, he was one of a kind, unique in so many ways. We didn't lose a pet; we lost a family member.

I always thought he depended on me, but I now know I relied on him just as much.

EVERYWHERE I look, I see traces of him, but he is nowhere to be found.

I feel alone for the first time in a very long time.
The house is quiet without him.
There is a void in my everyday life.
Some of my happiest memories are with him.
He was a gift, a blessing.
It will take me a long time to heal.

Although he may not be here in physical form, his sweet face is forever embedded in our hearts. He will never be forgotten.

This story shares just a few highlights of our unforgettable memories. I am honored to be able to share the story of such a beautiful, sweet soul. It was a privilege to be his mom.
"How lucky am I to have something that makes saying goodbye so hard" (Winnie the Pooh)

"Dogs ask for so little but deserve so much" (@everydayhowl)
Give your sweet fur babies an extra hug today.

"I think dogs are the most amazing creatures; they give unconditional love. For me, they are the role model for being alive." - Gilda Radner

Spike

SPIKE TO THE RESCUE

By Rox Burkey

I was a premature baby born during a blizzard in Illinois in December. At four pounds three ounces and fourteen and one-half inches long, my mom's doctor gave her a fifty percent chance I'd make it.

The hospital requirement for babies then was three days before they were released. Mom and Dad took me home at the time of release, hoping for the best.

They would take turns watching me in a makeshift bassinet lined with a blanket, better known as the dresser's top drawer. Squeaking at three-hour intervals, no crying, I was fed a few ounces of milk, changed, and returned to sleep.

Dad was an engineer for an airline, so after a couple of weeks, he returned to work. He was gone five days and back for three in rotation. My older brother would do some watching in the early evenings so Mom could take a nap. It was tough on them, but I didn't realize it then.

Following the Happy New Year, I was over a month old and gained two pounds, plus half an inch in length. I remained quiet, though I stayed awake for an hour, sometimes two, after eating.

Mom was ecstatic. When Dad returned from his trip, he added a family watchdog, a pure-bred Doberman named Spike.

He spent all his free time training Spike to stay in the unfenced yard and to provide guard duty. The object of his guarding was me.

He would lie on the floor by my drawer for hours, only going outside for puppy business and breakfast. If I had odd squeaks,

Spike would do low woofs to alert any close-by family member. Trust me, the house was small, and someone was always nearby. We were not rich, so each item acquired was well thought out and purchased based on its long-term usefulness.

The next few months continued the same regimen, with Spike supplementing my mom's watchful eyes.

At my six-month check-up with the pediatrician, I was given the green light to be put onto the floor to see if crawling was in my future.

Soft solids were introduced, and Spike was more than gracious, licking any excess falling off my fingers and the highchair tray. He was also the master at after-meal cleanup duty until Mom arrived with a warm washcloth.

At the ripe age of ten months, I finally began the backward boot scoot, which Spike would follow with fascination. I could lay on his stomach like a pillow when I got tired. He never moved first or caused my head to bounce on the floor. I gained enough weight to sleep eight hours at night and finally fit into my onesies shortly after my first birthday.

Dad's workdays were consistent during my first year and a half. He would train Spike with single-word and hand commands. Spike grew faster than me.

By my eighteenth month mark, he had one hundred ten pounds of muscle and teeth. Our magnificent red Doberman loved to smile and lick.

The other activity he loved when outdoors roaming our acre of property was finding stuff to chew. Not eating chewing, but making noise chomping, with empty oil cans the preferred item if the farm next to our property happened to toss one.

Spike had exploration limits at the front, east, or west of our property line. On the back side, flanked by the farmer, was fair territory. He would bring presents to Mom and leave them at the backdoor, like rodents, birds, or rotten fruit such as melons. She would reprimand him, and he'd sit or lay by me.

One day, I think he encouraged me to latch onto his back and try walking. I would grab his short hair and loose skin in my small hands with tenacious fingers, hanging on for dear life. After a few steps, the inevitable fall on the rump would happen, and we would begin again.

Mom said this routine continued for several weeks. When Dad returned from a trip, he was so delighted at my progress and Spike's gentle nature that he sat me on Spike's back and allowed me to ride him. Spike never protested, but Mom and my brother couldn't try this unless Dad was home.

All this walking stuff made me extra tired. Mom found me a bassinet on wheels, which, during the day, she would put me in to keep close by, especially if Spike was outside.

The Hawkeye Quality Baskenette on Wheels Burlington Basket was thirty-two inches long, twenty inches wide, and fifteen inches tall. I stayed in it most of the time, moving from room to room or outdoors based on what chores my mom was trying to complete. When my parents first received it, I slept in it in their room.

One chore Mom particularly disliked was washing clothes, ringing them out by hand, and then hanging them up on the outdoor clothesline. The clean laundry smelled fresh from clean air, but it was time-consuming work.

She had a crank washing machine but grumbled that drying items, particularly sheets during the long winters, was impossible. Dad found a used dryer somewhere and brought it home as a surprise after a flight.

He and a neighbor down the way wired it and put it into the designated laundry room. During the cooler fall weather, Mom decided it was the perfect place for me to be snuggled up for a midday nap in the Hawkeye.

A family of four, with one being a very active boy, had laundry. Dad's shirts required for his work with the airline were a constant wash and dry activity between trips. Those two appliances had quite the workout.

Three months before my second birthday, I was still reasonably small. Though steadier on my feet, I liked the comfort of my Hawkeye and never whined or cried to be taken out.

I was speaking a bit, but nothing unusual. Mom said I would often lie awake with my big blues open, observing the world. If I wasn't tired enough to sleep, I watched the world around me.

September was colder than usual. A cold front changed the leaves almost overnight. Mom wanted to finish the laundry before Dad arrived the next day so she could focus on his work clothes.

She started early and allowed me to stay in the laundry room. During the first two loads, she would talk and sing with me; we both sang flat but did not care.

The back wall had a rod to hang up clothes and a table for folding. She placed the third load of wash into the dryer and, noticing I was asleep, left me in the Hawkeye and went to the other side of the house to complete different chores and get things ready for supper. My brother also asked for help with his homework. The door between the laundry room and the rest of the house was ajar, and Spike was indoors.

They believe the wiring sparked fifteen or twenty minutes into the sixty-minute drying cycle. It sparked to the point that it set the lint accumulated on the back of the dryer aflame. The flame licked

133

the wooden paneling behind the appliances, also starting them on fire.

Spike woofed, but no one came. My Hawkeye was perpendicular to the inside door, so that intelligent pup took matters into his paws.

He pressed his one hundred-ten pounds, full force, against the outside door until it cracked and splintered open. He pushed the Hawkeye outdoors onto the patio moments before my mom rushed into the laundry room.

She grabbed the plug from the wall and used the fire extinguisher to extinguish the fire. Picking me up, she ran with Spike on her heels to the front door and got my brother out of the house.

Running next door, she called the fire department, who arrived within minutes. They said she did everything right. She told them Spike was the hero. Once Mom set me on the floor, Spike licked me and remained my best buddy for fifteen years.

Spike is the reason I survived that day.

"Ask me to show you poetry in motion, and I will show you a horse." - Author Unknown

Thunder

THE BLESSINGS OF THUNDER

By Marybeth Haines

"To ride a horse, is to ride the sky" – Author Unknown

Ever since I can remember, I've shared life with an animal, from living on a hobby farm with various barnyard creatures to furry beloved inside the home. These loving souls weren't just animals but teachers, healers, and guides.

When it came time for an animal friend to transition from physical form to spirit, as a child, I felt confused about the impermanence of our existence. I have memories of a special space where we would bury our pets after they passed, and together as a family, we would sing a song or say a prayer.

This area became what we would refer to as our pet cemetery for many years. I'm grateful for this experience because it taught me the importance of celebrating one's life.

Moving forward, many cats, dogs, rabbits, guinea pigs, fish, and frogs bring fond memories to my heart, and I remember the joys, sorrows, lessons, and celebrations I had with them. Each was a soul connection that helped me move through life in magnificent ways.

At age 10, I met a horse named Thunder with gorgeous grey fur and a stellar blonde mane. He came to live on our farm, and I remember braiding his hair while giving him fancy haircuts for his forelock. Oh, the things he let me do!

137

My childhood was challenging as my emotions were often far from what I could identify—not understanding what I felt made it difficult to maneuver through what was supposed to be fun childhood years.

It wouldn't be until some 40+ years later that I understood why I felt things so deeply back then, being a highly sensitive person.

When we experience events in life that are traumatic and stressful, we often feel stuck while we try to move through the healing. This was a pivotal time in my life, and Thunder became my teacher. He taught me how to find the strength for who I was becoming.

As a young girl transitioning through what I often refer to as the "in-between years" (I was not a young child anymore, but I was not quite a teenager yet), I felt the deep desire to become independent and stand in my strength. Above all, it was important to do this successfully.

In my 10-year-old mind, one way of achieving this goal was the quest of galloping on Thunder all by myself without anyone's help. I wanted to gallop with him freely and feel good inside a body that was hurting emotionally.

Usually, when Thunder and I rode together, my sister was present. This time, I wanted things to be different. So, I brought Thunder into the barn, we got saddled up, and ventured out into the backfield of 25 acres. I remember feeling a deep fear come over me. This was outside my comfort zone. But I knew only I could do this if I wanted to succeed.

Once we were in a good place on the land, I gave Thunder the command to begin trotting, and he responded in the unique way he always would. Trotting with him felt good, and I began to smile.

Galloping came next, and we shared an incredible connection during this moment. The wind blew through my hair, and we flowed in the freedom of the run. I remember thinking to myself, "I did it!" *"I'm doing it!"* and thanking Thunder for his gift of this ride.

It was a short-lived moment of bliss, and before I could fully realize what was happening, I found myself flying through the air and falling to the ground hard. I looked up to find where my friend Thunder was and saw that he was ahead of me in the distance with his saddle hanging off the side of his body.

The pain I felt was immense, and everything hurt. Once I observed his saddle in the manner it was hanging, I realized I hadn't saddled him properly, and with the movement of the gallop, it had slipped. I felt deep sadness and a feeling of failure. I told myself it was my fault this happened, and I was afraid to ride Thunder again.

I don't remember what happened after that. I may have blocked it out, and someone might have found us to bring us back to the barn. Regardless of the outcome, I never talked much about this afterward and chose to keep these emotions buried deep inside.

There are sayings about riding a horse: "If you fall off, you need to get back on" and "Get back up on the horse." Thunder was my teacher when I learned how to do this.

I didn't understand this event's gift until later in life. What happened that summer day wasn't about falling off my horse. It was a learning experience for me to grow through healing.

It carried a dual meaning and created an invitation to not only shift the fear I felt of being able to ride again (getting back up on Thunder) but also find how to identify the deep emotion inside that I had been holding onto for so many years from childhood trauma.

Although I never wanted to experience this event again, I believe it happened so that Thunder's role as a teacher could be activated.

He helped me get "back up on the horse" again and move through life in a new way that I was so desperately trying to find out how to do.

My time with this soul friend in equine form came to fruition, and after a little while, Thunder moved to his next adventure and new home.

His photo sits on my desk, and I look at it each day, remembering the joys of our time together. Throughout it all, Thunder remained my teacher in so many ways.

My time with Thunder was a gift, and I will always be grateful. I thank him for his kindness and holding of space, and my love for him will always be cherished. There's so much to tell you about this grey-furred, blonde-maned beauty named Thunder, and I hope sharing this story has given him the credit he deserves.

As I shared my story of a horse named Thunder and how he made an impression and a difference in my life, I now ask you about the animals in your life. How have they come here to help you?

Consider this to learn more about their gifts, why they've come, and what they've chosen to share with you!

It's true that "an animal's love is forever." Animals are our teachers, healers, and guides, bringing meaning to our experiences.

When we are open to receiving these gifts from them, we can finally say that our lives have been blessed. I don't know where I'd be without Thunder, and I thank him for being my friend.

"No one appreciates the very special genius of your conversation as the dog does."

Christopher Morley

Trevor

LIFE IN A DAY

By Charles Breakfield

Rachel dragged herself into the living room. Her long, blond ponytail, a signature of her carefree spirit, flew when she flumped onto the sofa. She was breathing hard, with fear for their beloved Doberman etched on her face. Mom looked on with concern.

"Mom, I've never seen Dad like that. It scared me to see him so frantic. Usually, nothing rattles him, but Dad had trouble speaking, trying to figure out what happened. Trevor was so weak and helpless, almost lifeless. Poor puppy didn't make a sound. Dad hurt his back, lifting the ninety-pound animal off the floor. We should have figured out something easier to get the dog into the car to take to the vet."

"It was heart-wrenching seeing poor Trevor struggling to get from his bed only to spin and collapse," admitted Mom, her voice trembling with emotion. "We barely managed to get him onto a soft blanket outside before he had another potty accident." Tears welled in her eyes. "Trevor was trying his best, but he was wobbling around like a leaf in a storm, his strength ebbing away. I was terrified, too."

On the verge of tears, Rachel said, "I don't know who I felt sorrier for, Trevor or Dad. I know you worked hours on the computer and phone to find a vet open on New Year's Day. I heard Dad yell he'd go to Oklahoma to find a clinic if he had to. I've never heard him use all those words he won't let us say all in one sentence."

"I've only seen him like that a couple of times. He gets completely unhinged when household members are sick or hurt. In this house, animals are family."

Rachel whispered, her voice choked with emotion, "I love Trevor. It crushed me to see him so frail and unable to move. He was perfectly fine last night. He's such a good boy."

"I never told you, but the same thing happened with Ronnie, the pretty female Pitbull we had before we found Trevor. Both dogs were castoffs your dad refused to turn away from rescuing. Ronnie was a jumper. No fence could hold her. A couple of times a week, if you weren't watching closely, she'd jump the fence and visit her best buddy, Sheba, down the street. Dad tried to make the fence jump-proof. She was always too clever until one time when she wasn't."

"What happened?"

Sandy sighed. "Once, she went over the fence to run and bark at the horses in the back pasture and didn't come back. Dad stormed around the neighborhood in the pickup, trying to locate her to bring her back. He was angry but scared she was gone forever. Dad hunted for her that afternoon and well into the evening. We had to go inside when it got dark, but we prayed she would return. The next morning, she was still missing. We were pretty sad."

Rachel's eyes threatened to overflow again. "I remember. That was horrible."

"Dad got up the next morning. He grabbed his ladder to climb over the fence, determined to walk every inch of the big pasture looking for her. I still laugh at what he found. Ronnie had jumped the fence, but one of her back legs got tangled up in the old rusty

145

fence and pinned her. She stood on three legs waiting to get rescued all night."

Rachel's eyes widened like saucers. "She was trapped by the fence the whole time. Why didn't she bark or whine so Dad could rescue her?"

"Ronnie wasn't a barker or whiner. Trevor's the same way. Dad hollered he'd found her and to bring some pliers. Once free, Dad gathered her in his arms and ran to the car, and we raced her to the vet. We got in right away."

"Dad couldn't do that for Trevor because everything was closed. No wonder he looked so worried."

"I got him an appointment, and Dad called after the vet saw Trevor. He said the people were nice and concerned, which helped. They gave Dad some meds for Trevor and said to take him to the regular vet tomorrow."

Bright and early the next day, they were all trying to load the Doberman into the backseat of the pickup truck for transport to the vet. Sandy and Rachel watched as Dad tried to move the struggling animal. It took all of them to get him in the pickup's back seat.

Once they got to the vet, Dad requested, "Rachel, go inside, please. See if they can send a technician to help me. I can't lift him anymore with my back like it is."

Rachel rushed in. Within minutes, a lone technician strolled out. Dad studied the man. "Where is the gurney? He is quite heavy."

The young man smirked. "I'm the gurney." Then he placed Trevor's front paws over his shoulder, scooped his hands under his bottom, and hefted the animal up like a baby—a big baby. After all the struggle between them, they were stunned at the sight.

Later that day, the vet called. "We have several scenarios in play with Trevor. We're not equipped to deal with them here. I've scheduled him with another specialty animal clinic north of town where you need to take him. Be here at three. I'll give you my analysis. North Texas Animal ER clinic already has it. I don't know the exact cause of the puppy's condition, but their state-of-the-art facilities can do more than we can."

Dad arrived on time, driving through worsening weather conditions, which made him feel down. The people at the North Texas Animal ER clinic were experienced professionals. No one wanted to leave him overnight, but the vet wanted to observe Trevor and wait for test results.

Dad asked, "Don't you have a magic wand to fix him up? We're used to having him around."

Dr. Chen smirked. "Sir, this requires exact science, lab work, and constant care to get him well. All of which we do for every patient we see. If we get a magic wand to heal the patients, I promise to use it."

He nodded. "Today is Wednesday. Please call us every day with a status update."

"Okay, but we need him to stay until at least Saturday."

"Three days without Trevor mooching food from the table or drooling slobber on the tile floor for us to slip on?" Sandy stomped her foot. "Say it isn't so."

Saturday finally arrived. The trio dashed to retrieve Trevor. They are relieved to find him markedly better and with prescriptions to administer for the next week.

Dad asked, "You ran a battery of tests. You've given him your best care and needed medication, so what was the problem?"

Dr. Chen offered a weak smile. "We don't know. We can treat the symptoms as situations arise, and he goes home and recovers. We all like Trevor. He is a very sweet boy, and we want to believe he will recover nicely over the next few weeks. We would like to see him again in six weeks."

Despite the cold outside, the doctor helped load Trevor into the truck and petted him for a few minutes.

Three weeks later, Trevor is mooching food from the table, drooling, and slobbering on the floor for people to slip on.

Dad remarked, "Trevor, I'm glad to have you home again," as he gave the big puppy a hug.

"If there are no dogs in heaven, then when I die I want to go where they went." - Will Rogers

Zach

ZACK THE LITTLE

By Bob Brill

From what I learned with Zach, the most frustrating thing about having a little, and I mean l-i-t-t-l-e dog, is that they are so hard to potty train. However, if I can toss that aside, I also learned Zach was the easiest dog to train about other stuff.

He walked without a leash, followed hand signals, and did what he was told via voice communication as if he were a human. This 12-pound Lilliputin was pretty amazing over his 15 years of life.

A pound rescue, it was my lucky day when I showed up at the Camarillo, CA shelter. I had gone there over the weekend, scouting out the pups beforehand. It had been long enough since I had to put down my previous rescue dog, and I wanted a puppy. When it came to puppies this day, there was one. Only one.

There he sat. He was this ugly Beagle/Boston mix who was all dwarf. He had very short legs, a brindle color, and gigantic eyes that asked, "Can I trust you?"

Well, this shelter only allowed puppies to be adopted on Tuesday mornings by lottery. You put your name on a piece of paper and put it in a can, and they'd draw a name from those who submitted their names. So, I went back a few days later for the drawing. It must have been providence.

Eight of us there wanted this little dog, barely eight weeks old, who had been abandoned wandering the streets of Oxnard. It was a rough beginning for the little guy. When my name was pulled, I couldn't believe it! I never win anything, but this time, I hit the jackpot.

This started a new life for Zacharius Brill, who would now be known as Zach. I must tell you I had three offers for Zach before I left the building, but I'd just won the lottery. You couldn't pry him away from me.

One couple wanted him as a companion for their German Shepherd. Really? Another didn't say, but a third wanted the dog for her child. As it turns out, that would not have been a good match. Zach realized how little he was and that he wasn't fond of kids.

They always wanted to pick him up. And with Zach, you had to pick him up gently, under the chest, and a second hand underneath his butt. He'd yelp loudly and even snap if you tried to pick him up under his front legs.

If you are wondering about the name, I've always tried to honor the Good Lord by naming my pets after Old Testament biblical characters. Laying hands on the dog, I asked for a loving pet who would become a part of the family. It always worked. Thank you.

My previous canines were Joshua and Mariah. Joshua was abandoned, so "Joshua the son of Nun" seemed appropriate. (Deuteronomy 34:9 ASV). And a female whom we named Mariah.

Ruth didn't seem like a good name for a dog, especially with the joke: "Did you know my dog can speak? Sure, he looked up at the top of the house and said Roof." It's a Stupid joke, but I could see I'd be hearing it if we named the dog Ruth. So, we went for Mariah, which I reasoned was a form of Miriam, Moses' sister. Okay, it's a stretch, but it was *my* dog.

While it was a frustrating time of housebreaking, this little guy would walk with me off the leash by my side. Attempting to cross the street, he obeyed hand signals with complete trust. It's not something encouraged these days, but seeing such obedience in an animal at the time was shocking. Because of this, I was confident in taking him for a walk any time of the day. When my new wife came into my life, she made me realize I did have to keep him on a leash, which I understood, and the walking voice commands stopped.

Zach wasn't the kind of dog who cuddled up with you. He did change when I was going through a divorce from my first wife. People say dogs feel your moods. He certainly did with me during that time. He'd lay between my legs down around my knees as I sat and watched TV or read sitting on the couch.

Later on, he began to change and didn't want any part of cuddling. I could not figure that out. Maybe my moods were changing, and what he sensed wasn't correct. I don't know.

Zach worked in my retail store (a mom-and-pop baseball card store at the time). He greeted customers, didn't care for kids, and starred in my TV commercials. You can find them on YouTube.

He had a very particular and strange talent; Zach could shoot (literally shoot) a paddle ball out of his mouth up to 10 feet! His owner was smart enough to recognize this talent and videotaped him often. The newer and firmer those little blue paddle balls were, the farther he'd shoot them. He would position them in his front bulldog teeth and squeeze. "Pop!" The ball would go flying.

I posted the best one on my YouTube channel. I set up a series of plastic bottles in a pyramid and lined up Zach to shoot them down. After a couple of misses, at my instruction, he repositioned himself, and bang! They went flying.

I wanted to get him on Stupid Pet Tricks and even submitted the video to America's Funniest Videos, but they never aired. This was an amazing talent he held until shortly before I had to make that final decision pet owners dread.

Zach was far from perfect. As frustrating as potty training was, there were times when he got downright obstinate toward the end. I remember one time he was particularly disobedient.

During the last year of his life, he and I were on the front porch when he decided to leave home. I called him, and he continued down the path of our condo complex. Running away from home was in his mind, I'm sure.

I stood up from my chair and yelled, "Zach, come back here!" It was as if he chose not to hear me—that whole selective hearing thing. I decided to go after him, walking and calling him. I knew better than to run because he'd run. Then he sped up, so I had to join the chase. He turned the corner, and I followed. Luckily, he turned another corner back toward the center of the complex. I don't know what I would have done if he headed out the open gate.

Finally, he worked his way toward a grassy area, looking back to see where I was. I knew he knew that I was as angry as I could be. Then I caught up with his little butt and dove, tackled him, and he chose to fight back. He snapped at me and bit me.

When I could corral him and pick him up, I had to keep my hand over his face and snout. There was no way he was going to bite me again. It was then I realized Zach was nearing the end. Something wasn't right. It would be another year before the decision was made. It turns out he had a sizeable growth (the size of an orange in a 12-pound body) in his gut.

Surgery at 15 years old was not a real option. I made a tough decision. As the time arrived to say goodbye, Zach looked up at me and licked my hand. The Vet said he was saying, "Let me go; it's time." It helped.

Zach was an incredible animal. I occasionally see or hear him walking through the house in the middle of the night. It's good to know that he still likes being around me. I certainly miss him.

Deuteronomy 34:9 American Standard Version (ASV)

"You can usually tell that a man is good if he has a dog who loves him."

W. Bruce Cameron

Zoey

LEAVING PAW PRINTS ON OUR SOULS

By Ann Brown

"I think it's time."

As a family, we lost our Lady in November 2021, the Sunday after Thanksgiving. The day after, I was able to move back into my house after a six-month bedroom and bathroom remodel due to mold.

Lady was almost 16, a Shih Tzu with all the typical breed issues. She had health problems as she aged and ended up needing 24/7 supervision for her safety, including hand feeding and directing her path since her vision had deteriorated.

I spent six months living with her, my parents, and my sister, which was a blessing amid the trials of dealing with black mold.

But a house isn't a home without paw prints.

Lady had left her paw prints on our hearts, and we knew she had crossed the rainbow bridge and joined my grandparents, her first family. She had been the last connection to them. It does take time to heal all wounds, but a dog-less house is hard.

"A dog is the only thing on earth that loves you more than he loves itself." Josh Billings

We were missing that unconditional love. My mom especially had the urge to fill that hole. My sister checked shelter posts and websites daily, especially the ANNA Shelter of Erie.

They listed Reggie, a Shih Tzu, one day in February. Although we have had female dogs in the past, we were open to meeting Reggie, a male. Our parents went to the shelter that day. The parking lot was filled with people wanting to meet the dogs.

Well, Reggie didn't work out. He didn't exist; he was a generic listing to tell the public that small dogs were available for adoption. However, they did have Malshipoo puppies they had rescued from a house of 17 dogs!

"Malshi-what?"

A mutt, as my dad says. No, an expensive, designer dog! Maltese, Shih Tzu and Poodle. "Do you have any females?"

Yes, they had one female. A scared, big-eyed Zoey. Her freshly groomed black and white fur made those eyes stick out even more. Well, she fell in love and adopted my mom right away. And she is still her human, although she's learned to tolerate the rest of us.

Blurry pictures were sent that day, asking what we thought about her.

"What do you think?" was our reply.

"Well, she's coming home with us!"

We'd just met our new fur-sister.

Zoey was officially adopted that day and made the scary trip home in the arms of my mom. She met me first. She was not impressed.

The next few days were an adjustment for all of us. We hadn't had a puppy in 16 years, and Zoey was seven months old. However, it would take some time for the puppy in her to come out. She had obliviously had some trauma and developed trust issues.

Zoey doesn't like men who wear black clothing or hats. Put them together, and it's full breaks on and barking. It took six months before my sister could go near her and 14 months before she'd let her pick her up.

We worked to gain her trust through feeding her and, of course, treats. Now, Zoey has trained my sister to give her the proper number of treats.

Zoey didn't know how to play. It took time and demonstration for her to learn. Imagine an adult; that would be me on the floor, playing alone. Now she loves her squeaky balls, especially if my sister tries to sleep!

Walks, or strolls, as I call them, were also a challenge at first. She had to figure out the leash and that she couldn't keep jumping up onto the cement retaining wall along the sidewalk.

Now, she reluctantly puts her harness on one paw at a time, lifting the right leg and then the left, with a "Do I really have to do this?" look on her face.

She loves to sniff every blade of grass and is excellent at helping to pull weeds in the summer. Most of the time, the evidence still hangs out of her mouth. But her favorite thing to sniff is the chocolate bunny jellybeans in the backyard.

Zoey's spunky personality has finally come out. She goes crazy when my mom returns, having been forced to nap on the couch while she waits for her return, even if she isn't left alone!

Her napping positions constantly change, but her favorite is all four legs in the air with her head on her pillow (which was supposed to be my dad's!)

Each part of her breed shows through in her personality and looks. Her coat is black and white. When it gets wet, the curl from the poodle comes out. She has wavy-haired ears and eyes that penetrate straight to your soul.

She also uses those puppy eyes to the max. She is too cute to resist and gets her way. I must say, though, she is not spoiled; she is just well-loved.

So, what is a Malshipoo? Maltese, Shih Tzu, and Poodle.

The Maltese is in her face and her loyalty. She constantly needs to be on a lap and is most content in my mom's lap, staring contently at her with her paws wrapped around her arm and looking around at the rest of us with that penetrating stare.

However, she does make her rounds. She loves ear rubs from me, and tummy rubs from our dad every morning and gives out high fives. My sister, with whom she also shares a birthday, can touch her freely now, but at the beginning, a treat payment was needed!

The Shih Tzu part of her comes through; she is a picky eater, scared of things, and so untrusting at times. On walks, Zoey often must be reassured and reminded to put her tail up and walk proudly. Her food needs to be specifically made, and then she must have the right conditions to eat in. This may partly be because of her not-so-pleasant experiences as a puppy in a house of 17 dogs!

The poodle smarts are where Zoey has the whole family well trained. We initially thought we were teaching her but quickly realized she was training us. We each have a different routine when giving her potty treats. And yes, she can count. She knows the number of treats she is supposed to get before bed so she can sleep properly. And she will let my parents know if they counted wrong, full puppy eyes if needed, but usually through paw waving and nose nudges.

Zoey is unafraid to let you know she is there and needs something, especially if you forget her potty treat. Like the rest of us, she has a routine and likes to stick to it.

A nudge to the leg with her nose. I need your attention. Mom just went into the bathroom; she nudges her nose around the door to ensure she's still there. I leave after supper, and she goes straight for her toys to play.

"It's amazing how much love and laughter they (dogs) bring into our lives and even how much closer we become with each other because of them." - John Grogan

This quote is 100% true. Zoey has been the glue that brought our family closer together. We laugh at her antics and how she wants to give so much love. How she tries to nip at my uncle's heels as he leaves, still not 100% trusting of him since he is usually dressed in black.

Joy as she looks fondly into my mother's eyes and lounges so relaxed and content in her arms. She can stare so intensely at you that you feel like she's penetrating your soul, forming a bond and understanding between you. The unconditional love of a pet is amazing; the love from Zoey is priceless.

Her personality is the sweetest and so loving—sometimes too loving. She always tries to give kisses, ensuring everyone knows how much love she must give.

I joke and say we should have renamed her Frogger because her tongue is so busy. We have given her many nicknames: ZoZo, ZoZo Bean, and Zoe-enator, to name a few.

She has been a huge blessing to our family, filling a hole and the need for paw prints in the house. We are well-loved, as is she.

Oh, and she is famous on six continents as she appears online, bringing joy to my sister's online students. She has her own page on ZooKidsReading.com and her own YouTube channel, Zoey's Ed-ventures!

We are so grateful that God thought of us, and Zoey decided to adopt us and leave her paw prints on our souls.

CONCLUSION

As we come to the end of "Paw Prints on the Kitchen Floor," it's clear that the bond between humans and their pets is extraordinary.

Each story shared has shown the unique ways in which our furry friends enrich our lives, bringing joy, comfort, and laughter, even amid tears.

Through the highs and lows, our pets have stood by our side with loyalty and unconditional love. They've taught us valuable lessons in compassion, patience, and resilience. Whether it's a wagging tail greeting us after a long day, a purring friend snuggling up on the couch or a friendly snort from your horse as you enter the barn in the morning. The presence of a pet transforms our daily lives in ways we could never have imagined.

Adopting or rescuing a pet is a profound act of kindness that reverberates far beyond the moment of bringing them home. Not only does it give a deserving animal a second chance at a happy life, but it brings immeasurable rewards to the adopter.

Each story reminds us to cherish the small moments, to find joy in the simple things, and to love unconditionally. As you turn the final page, may you carry with you the paw prints left on your heart by these touching tales.

And if you ever find yourself with the opportunity to welcome a pet into your life, may you embrace it wholeheartedly, knowing that the love you give will be returned tenfold.

Thank you for joining us on this journey through the lives of our beloved pets and their humans.

The next few pages are filled with practical advice for the new pet parent.

Things to consider before you get a pet.

When choosing your family's pet, you should know what type of pet you want.

Several factors should go into making that decision.

* How old are your kids?

* How many people are in the house?

* How much time do you have?

* How much space do you have?

* How much energy do you have?

* Do you have the financial resources to care for a pet?

Owning a pet is a privilege that brings great rewards. However, because our pets can't speak for themselves, we must each take on the responsibility as owners to advocate for them and provide the support and resources they need to live healthy, happy lives.

Providing that support begins even before we bring a pet home.

Source – AVMA (American Veterinary Medical Association)

There are many reasons to have a pet in your life. So we don't create an entire book of good reasons (but we could!), here are five reasons why having a pet is beneficial to your life:

Companionship and Emotional Support: Pets, whether dogs, cats, or even smaller animals such as rabbits or birds, bring unique joy and happiness to your life. They provide companionship that can significantly improve your emotional well-being. They offer unconditional love, reduce loneliness, and can even help alleviate symptoms of anxiety and depression.

According to research from Harvard Health Publishing, interacting with pets can increase levels of the hormone oxytocin, known as the "love hormone," which helps reduce stress and improve mood.

Source: https://www.health.harvard.edu

Physical Health Benefits: Owning a pet often encourages physical activity and outdoor time, especially with dogs that require regular walks or playtime. This increased exercise can lead to better cardiovascular health, lower blood pressure, and reduced cholesterol levels. Studies reported by the CDC (Centers for Disease Control and Prevention) suggest that pet owners tend to have lower blood pressure and cholesterol levels, which can lower the risk of heart disease.

Source: https://www.cdc.gov/healthypets/health-benefits/index.html

Stress Relief: Pets are natural stress relievers. Spending time with a pet, such as petting or playing with them, can help reduce cortisol levels (a stress-related hormone) and promote relaxation. This can have a calming effect on your overall mood and help you cope with daily stresses more effectively.

Source: https://www.mayoclinic.org/healthy-lifestyle

Social Connection: Pets can also facilitate social interactions and help you connect with others. Whether you're walking your dog in the park or chatting with other pet owners at the vet, pets provide a common ground for conversation and can help you meet new people. This social support network can contribute to a sense of belonging and improve mental health.

Purpose and Routine: Taking care of a pet gives you a sense of purpose and routine. Pets rely on you for their daily needs, such as feeding, grooming, and exercise. This responsibility can structure your day, increase self-discipline, and boost feelings of accomplishment. It can also benefit young adults transitioning into more independent living situations.

Overall, having a pet can enrich your life in many ways, from emotional support and improved physical health to fostering social connections and providing a sense of purpose. Whether you're considering getting a pet or already have one, these benefits highlight their positive impact on your well-being.

What other benefits can you think of from your own experience?

Adopting a pet is an exciting decision that comes with responsibilities. To ensure your new furry family member feels welcomed and comfortable in their new home, here is a list of items you'll want to have ready <u>before</u> bringing them home:

Food and Water Bowls: Choose sturdy, non-tip bowls right for your pet's size. Stainless steel is a good choice.

Quality Pet Food: Research and select a nutritious diet suitable for your pet's age, breed, and health needs.

Collar and Leash (for dogs): These are essential for walks and identification tags. Make sure the collar fits snugly but comfortably.

Bedding: Provide a cozy bed or blanket where your pet can rest undisturbed.

Toys: Keep your pet entertained and mentally stimulated with toys appropriate for their size and preferences.

Grooming Supplies: Depending on your pet, grooming supplies may include brushes, nail clippers, toothbrushes, and shampoo.

Litter Box and Litter (for cats): If you adopt a cat, ensure you have a litter box that suits its size and preferences, along with litter.

Scratching Post (for cats): Helps fulfill their natural scratching instincts and keeps their claws healthy.

Pet Carrier: This is essential for transporting your pet safely, whether it's for trips to the vet or travel.

Identification Tags and Microchip: Ensure your pet can be identified in case it runs off or gets lost.

Having these items ready before bringing your pet home helps ensure a smooth transition and helps them settle into their new environment comfortably. It also shows your commitment to their well-being from the start. Every pet is unique, so tailor your choices to their needs and personality.

Your new furry family member is home. Now what?

<u>**A good rule of thumb to follow is the 3 – 3 – 3 Rule.**</u>

The "3-3-3 rule" is a guideline often referenced when bringing an adopted pet home, particularly for dogs, though it can apply broadly to various pets. Here's what it generally entails:

First 3 Days: The initial days are crucial for your new pet to acclimate to their new surroundings. Expect them to feel anxious or stressed as they adapt to the change. During this time:

- **Quiet Environment:** Keep noise and activity levels low to reduce stress.

- **Introduction:** Introduce them gradually to family members and other pets, if applicable, calmly.

- **Basic Needs:** Focus on establishing routines for feeding, potty breaks, and sleep.

First 3 Weeks: As your pet settles in, you may notice their personality emerging more clearly. During this phase:

- **Bonding Time:** Spend quality time bonding with your pet through gentle interactions, playtime, and positive reinforcement training.

- **Routine and Stability:** Continue establishing a consistent daily routine to help them feel secure.

- **Training and Socialization:** Begin basic training and socialization efforts based on your pet's needs and comfort level.

First 3 Months: Your pet should begin to feel more comfortable and secure in their new home. However, remember:

- **Patience and Understanding:** Some behaviors may still require adjustment. Be patient and understanding as your pet continues to settle.

- **Health and Wellness:** Ensure regular vet check-ups, maintain a healthy diet and meet grooming needs.

- **Building Trust:** Continue building trust and a strong bond through positive interactions and consistent care.

The 3-3-3 rule reminds us that **patience, consistency, and understanding** are key when welcoming a new pet into your home.

Every pet adjusts at its own pace. Allow them time to settle in. A nurturing environment is essential for their well-being and establishing a solid bond with you and your family.

Thank you for reading this book!

If you enjoyed it, consider **leaving a review** on Amazon.

Other ways to help get the word out:

- Share a link to the book or share it on social media.
- Pick up another copy to share with someone.
- Recommend this book.

Remember, with each purchase, you are helping to support a worthy, no-kill animal shelter!

Meet the Coordinator and Lead Author of this book

Kim Lengling

Amazon Author Page: https://amzn.to/3RIMIc2

Website: https://www.kimlenglingauthor.com

Let Fear Bounce Podcast: https://anchor.fm/kim-lengling1

Facebook: https://www.facebook.com/letfearbouncepodcast

LinkedIn: https://www.linkedin.com/in/kimberlylengling/

Instagram: https://www.instagram.com/lenglingauthor/

Twitter: https://twitter.com/KimLengling

Want to find more good reads?
Connect with co-authors of this book!

Randi-Lee Bowslaugh
https://www.rbwriting.ca

Charles Breakfield
https://www.enigmabookseries.com/

Bob Brill
https://bobbrillbooks.com/

Ann Brown
http://zookidsreading.com/

Roxanne Burkey
https://www.enigmabookseries.com/

Anna Carranza
https://www.annacarranza.com

Carrie Carter
https://carriecarterwrites.com/

Marybeth Haines
https://www.thegalspeaks.com
https://www.harmoniceggniagara.com

Lori Keesey
https://lorikeesey.com

Maureen Scanlon
https://lifecoachmaureen.com/

Quote Sources:

https://www.care.com/c/the-101-best-dog-quotes
https://www.mahimahorseriding
https://living.greatpetcare.com/
https://ridetheskyequine.com/
https://www.azquotes.com/
https://www.countryliving.com/
https://www.brainyquote.com/quotes

Made in the USA
Monee, IL
29 August 2024

64879027R00098